D0908746

FOREVER
AND
Anon

anonymous /ə-non'i-məs/ adj lacking a name; without
name of author, real or feigned; lacking distinctive
features or individuality. [Gr *anōnymos*, from an-
(privative), and onyma, onoma name]

FOREVER
AND
Anon

A Treasury of Poetry
and Prose from the Pen of
AUTHOR UNKNOWN

COMPILED BY
GERRY HANSON

BOOKS

For Jill, who, happily, is anything but anonymous, with my love.

First published in Great Britain in 2007 by JR Books, 10 Greenland Street, London NW1 9ND www.jrbooks.com

Compilation copyright © 2007 Gerry Hanson

Gerry Hanson has asserted his moral right to be identified as the Author of this Work in accordance with the Copyright Designs and Patents Act 1998.

A catalogue record for this book is available from the British Library.

ISBN 978 1 906217 11 2

1 3 5 7 9 10 8 6 4 2

Printed by MPG Books, Bodmin, Cornwall

Every effort has been made by the author to trace and check the anonymity of the poems and prose contained herein.

CONTENTS

Introduction

Most poetry benefits from being read aloud, whether to oneself or to an audience. In his poem 'The Day is Done', Henry Wadsworth Longfellow encouraged the reading aloud of poetry as a way of banishing the cares of the day, but he urged us to read 'Not from the grand old masters/Not from the bards sublime', but instead to 'Read from some humbler poet/Whose songs gushed from his heart/As showers from the clouds of summer,/Or tears from the eyelids start'.

Whether the poems in this collection are by grand old masters or by humbler poets, they have one thing in common: they have all become disconnected from their creators. How it is that we do not know who wrote, 'Greensleeves', 'The British Grenadiers', 'The Vicar of Bray', and 'Here's a Health unto his Majesty' is a mystery. An even greater mystery is how we have been singing the words of our national anthem for more than 250 years and yet no one has the faintest idea who wrote them. I have included all three original verses, even though verse two, ('O Lord our God arise, scatter our enemies and make them fall'), has been dropped from most hymn-books as being too belligerent. I fail to understand why. How can it be wrong to ask God to make our enemies fall? And if verse two is unacceptable, we surely shouldn't be singing the first verse which asks God to, 'send her victorious'. How can He send her victorious if our enemies do *not* fall? If we are forbidden to sing verse two, it is entirely appropriate that it ends, 'God save us all!'

When seeking a title, Maureen Lipman suggested 'Anon – The Canon', but to justify such a title would require several volumes, for there is so much material to choose from. (I have been happy to use Maureen's other suggestion, 'Anon-de-script', as the title of the final section). As with my previous book, *England, my England*, the biggest problem was not what to put in, but what to leave out. I have endeavoured to strike a balance between the familiar and the unfamiliar and between the profound and the frivolous. Above all, I have tried to produce a book that readers will enjoy dipping into and which meets Longfellow's suggestion to

>...read from the treasured volume
>The poem of thy choice,
>And lend to the rhyme of the poet
>The beauty of thy voice.
>And the night shall be filled with music
>And the cares that infest the day
>Shall fold their tents, like the Arabs,
>And as silently steal away.

If this book succeeds in soothing a few cares, I'll be exceedingly gruntled.

Acknowledgements

During the period I was compiling this anthology, The Poetry Library was closed while its home, the Royal Festival Hall, was being refurbished, and I very much missed that valuable resource and its ever-helpful staff. I was all the more grateful, therefore, to the many friends who delved into old files and searched the backs of desk drawers to provide me with items to augment those I found in various other libaries and from trawling through my own collection of more than a hundred anthologies.

To steal from one person's work is plagiarism, but to steal from several is research! I am particularly grateful to Mary Bolton, Amy Cockett, Rita Gilpin, Marion Griffin and John Robinson, who allowed me to 'steal' from their items, and to the Reverend John Wynburne, whose two excellent books of readings for weddings and funerals were a useful source of material.

My thanks to the ever-helpful Melanie Letts, who so efficiently and accurately organised the text, and to my editor, Lesley Wilson, whose patience and wise guidance I greatly appreciate. Thank you, also, to Richard Mason, for the design. Most of all, however, my thanks to Jeremy Robson, who encouraged me to compile this collection of the work of the world's most prolific poet.

Gerry Hanson

TIME LIKE AN
EVER-ROLLING STREAM

THE LOOM OF TIME

Man's life is laid in the loom of time
    To a pattern he does not see,
While the weavers work and the shuttles fly
    Till the dawn of eternity.

Some shuttles are filled with silver threads
    And some with threads of gold,
While often but the darker hues
Are all that they may hold.

But the weaver watches with skilful eye
    Each shuttle fly to and fro,
And sees the pattern so deftly wrought
    As the loom moves sure and slow.

God surely planned the pattern:
    Each thread, the dark and fair,
Is chosen by His master skill
    And placed in the web with care.

He only knows its beauty,
    And guides the shuttles which hold

The threads so unattractive,
    As well as the threads of gold.

Not till each loom is silent,
    And the shuttles cease to fly,
Shall God reveal the pattern
    And explain the reason why

The dark threads were as needful
    In the weaver's skilful hand
As the threads of gold and silver
    For the pattern which He planned.

TAKE TIME

Take time to THINK
    it is the source of power.
Take time to PLAY
    it is the secret of perpetual youth.
Take time to READ
    it is the fountain of wisdom.
Take time to PRAY
    it is the greatest power on earth.
Take time to LOVE and BE LOVED
    it is God's greatest gift.
Take time to BE FRIENDLY
    it is the road to happiness.
Take time to LAUGH
    it is the music of the soul.

Take time to GIVE
    it is too short a day to be selfish.
Take time to WORK
    it is the price of success.
Take time to BE CHARITABLE
    it is the key to heaven.

MAKE THE MOST OF TODAY

To realise the value of ONE YEAR, ask a student who
    failed a grade.
To realise the value of ONE MONTH, ask a mother
    who gave birth to a premature baby.
To realise the value of ONE WEEK, ask the editor of
    a weekly newspaper.
To realise the value of ONE HOUR, ask the lovers
    who are waiting to meet.
To realise the value of ONE MINUTE, ask a person
    who has just missed a train.
To realise the value of ONE SECOND, ask a person
    who has just avoided an accident.
To realise the value of ONE MILLISECOND, ask a
    person who won a silver medal in the Olympics.
Treasure every moment that you have! Treasure it
    more because you shared it with someone special.
Tomorrow is a mystery. Today is a gift – that's why it
    is called THE PRESENT.

TIME

Time is …
>Too Slow for those who Wait,
>Too Swift for those who Fear,
>Too Long for those who Grieve,
>Too Short for those who Rejoice,
But for those who Love,
>Time is Eternity.

THE INN OF LIFE

Life's like an inn where travellers stay,
Some only breakfast and then go away;
Others to dinner stay and are full-fed,
The oldest only sup and go to bed;
Long is his bill who lingers out the day,
Who goes the soonest has the least to pay.

LOOK TO THIS DAY, FOR IT IS LIFE

    Look to this day,
For it is life, the very life of life.
In its brief course lie all the
Varieties and realities of your existence:
    The bliss of growth,
    The glory of action,
    The splendour of beauty;
For yesterday is but a dream
And tomorrow is only a vision,
    But today well lived makes
Every yesterday a dream of happiness,
And every tomorrow a vision of hope.
    Look well therefore to this day!
    Such is the salutation of the dawn.

CHINESE PROVERB

If there is right in the soul
There will be beauty in the person
if there is beauty in the person
There will be harmony in the home
If there is harmony in the home
There will be peace in the world.

THE DIVINE WEAVER

Our lives are but a weaving
Between our Lord and we;
We cannot choose the colours
He weaves so steadily.
Often He weaves in sorrow
But we in foolish pride
Forget He sees the upper,
And we, the lower side.
But the dark threads are as needful
In the weaver's skilful hand
As the threads of gold and silver
In the pattern He has planned.
Not till the loom is silent
And the bobbins cease to fly,
Shall He unroll the canvas
And explain the reason why.

OUR CHOICE

Not what we have, but what we are.
Not what we see, but what we choose.
These are the things that mar or bless,
The sum of human happiness.

The thing nearby, not that afar.
Not what we seem, but what we are.
These are the things that make or break,
That give the heart its joy or ache.

Not what seems fair, but what is true.
Not what we dream, but what we do.
These are the things that shine like gems,
Like stars in fortune's diadems.

Not as we take, but as we give.
Not as we pray, but as we live.
These are the things that make for peace,
Both now and after time shall cease.

THE COLOUR OF YOUR LIFE

If you painted your life, would it mostly be grey?
With rare flames of scarlet for each special day
And of strands of silver where you kept your illusions
Mixed in with the blues showing loss and confusion.

If you painted your life, would there be storms?
For the times you lost courage and agreed to conform
Perhaps you'd paint stars, one for each dream
That gave life a meaning, or so once it seemed.

Has anyone else painted clouds in your sky?
And dulled your bright colours as your chances
passed by?
Maybe it's time to take back the brush,
Start painting your own life, enough is enough.

You can paint rainbows, banishing grey
And splash on some gold, starting today.
Puddles of silver: shimmering, bright;
Walk out of the shadows, come into the light.

Perhaps you need mellow, golden nut-brown
Are you running too fast, is it time to slow down?
Paint yourself peace and space just to be,
Gentle blue mornings, a soft lilac sea.

In your painting of life let the beautiful days
Shimmer in gold and light up the greys.
Paint it with courage, thread silver strands,
Pick up your brush, life's in your own hands.

CHILDREN

If children live with criticism
    they learn to condemn
If children live with hostility
    they learn to fight
If children live with ridicule
    they learn to be shy
If children live with shame
    they learn to feel guilty
If children live with tolerance
    thy learn to be patient
If children live with encouragement
    they learn confidence
If children live with praise
    they learn to appreciate
If children live with fairness
    they learn justice
If children live with security
    they learn to have faith
If children live with approval
    they learn to like themselves
If children live with acceptance and friendship
    they learn to find love in the world

THE HUMAN CONDITION

SHE WAS POOR BUT SHE WAS HONEST

SHE was poor but she was honest,
> Victim of a rich man's game;
First he loved her, then he left her,
> And she lost her maiden name.

Then she hastened up to London,
> For to hide her grief and shame;
There she met another rich man,
> And she lost her name again.

See her riding in her carriage,
> In the Park and all so gay;
All the nibs and nobby persons
> Come to pass the time of day.

See them at the gay theatre
> Sitting in the costly stalls;
With one hand she holds the programme,
> With the other strokes his hand.

See him have her dance in Paris
> In her frilly underclothes;

All those Frenchies there applauding
 When she strikes a striking pose.

See the little country village
 Where her aged parents live;
Though they drink champagne she sends them,
 Still they never can forgive.

In the rich man's arms she flutters
 Like a bird with a broken wing;
First he loved her, then he left her,
 And she hasn't got a ring.

See him in his splendid mansion
 Entertaining with the best,
While the girl as he has ruined
 Entertains a sordid guest.

See him riding in his carriage
 Past the gutter where she stands;
He has made a stylish marriage
 While she wrings her ringless hands.

See him in the House of Commons
 Passing laws to put down crime,
While the victim of his passions
 Slinks away to hide her shame.

See her on the bridge at midnight
 Crying, 'Farewell, faithless love!'
There's a scream, a splash – Good Heavens!
 What is she a-doing of?

Then they dragged her from the river,
    Water from her clothes they wrung;
They all thought that she was drownded,
    But the corpse got up and sung:

'It's the same the whole world over;
    It's the poor as gets the blame,
It's the rich as gets the pleasure –
    Ain't it all a bleeding shame!'

AN ORIGINAL LOVE STORY

He struggled to kiss her. She struggled the same
    To prevent him so bold and undaunted;
But, as smitten by lightning, he heard her exclaim,
    'Avaunt, Sir!' and off he avaunted.

But when he returned, with the fiendishest laugh,
    Showing clearly that he was affronted,
And threatened by main force to carry her off,
    She cried 'Don't!' and the poor fellow donted.

When he meekly approached, and sat down at her feet,
    Praying aloud, as before he had ranted,
That she would forgive him and try to be sweet,
    And said 'Can't you!' the dear girl recanted.

Then softly he whispered, 'How could you do so?
    I certainly thought I was jilted;
But come thou with me, to the parson we'll go;
    Say, wilt thou, my dear?' and she wilted.

POLLY, PUT THE KETTLE ON

Polly, put the kettle on,
Polly, put the kettle on,
Polly, put the kettle on:
We'll all have tea.

Sukey, take it off again,
Sukey, take it off again,
Sukey, take it off again:
They've all gone away.

POLLY PERKINS

I am a broken-hearted milkman, in grief I'm arrayed,
Through keeping of the company of a young
    servant maid,
Who lived on board and wages the house to keep clean
In a gentleman's family near Paddington Green.

    Chorus:
        She was as beautiful as a butterfly
        And as proud as a Queen
        Was pretty little Polly Perkins of
        Paddington Green.

She'd an ankle like an antelope and a step like a deer,
A voice like a blackbird, so mellow and clear,
Her hair hung in ringlets so beautiful and long,
I thought that she loved me but I found I was wrong.

When I'd rattle in a morning and cry 'milk below',
At the sound of my milk-cans her face she would show
With a smile upon her countenance and a laugh in
     her eye,
If I thought she'd have loved me, I'd have laid down
     to die.

When I asked her to marry me she said 'Oh! What stuff',
And told me to 'drop it, for she had quite enough
Of my nonsense' – at the same time I'd been very kind,
But to marry a milkman she didn't feel inclined.

'Oh, the man that has me must have silver and gold,
A chariot to ride in and be handsome and bold,
His hair must be curly as any watch spring,
And his whiskers as big as a brush for clothing.'

The words that she uttered went straight through
     my heart,
I sobbed and I sighed, and straight did depart;
With a tear on my eyelid as big as a bean,
Bidding good-bye to Polly and Paddington Green.

In six months she married, – this hard-hearted girl, -
But it was not a Wi-count, and it was not a Nearl,
It was not a 'Baronite', but a shade or two wuss,
It was a bow-legged conductor of a twopenny bus.

UNFORTUNATE MISS BAILEY

A captain bold from Halifax who dwelt in
    country quarters,
Betrayed a maid who hanged herself one morning in
    her Garters.
His wicked conscience smited him, he lost his
    Stomach daily,
And took to drinking Ratafia while thinking of
    Miss Bailey.
One night betimes he went to bed, for he had caught
    a Fever;
Says he, 'I am a handsome man, but I'm a gay Deceiver.'
His candle just at twelve o'clock began to burn
    quite palely,
A Ghost stepped up to his bedside and said 'Behold
    Miss Bailey!'
'Avaunt, Miss Bailey!' then he cries, 'your Face looks
    white and mealy.'
'Dear Captain Smith,' the ghost replied, 'you've used
    me ungenteelly;
The Crowner's 'Quest goes hard with me because I've
    acted frailly,
And Parson Biggs won't bury me though I am dead
    Miss Bailey.'

'Dear Corpse!' said he, 'since you and I accounts
    must once for all close,
There really is a one-pound note in my regimental
    Small-clothes;
I'll bribe the sexton for your grave.' The ghost then
    vanished gaily
Crying, 'Bless you, Wicked Captain Smith, Remember
    poor Miss Bailey.'

THE FOGGY, FOGGY DEW

When I was a bachelor, I lived by myself
And I worked at the weaver's trade;
The only, only thing that I ever did wrong
Was to woo a fair young maid.
I wooed her in the winter time,
And in the summer, too;
And the only, only thing that I ever did wrong
Was to keep her from the foggy, foggy dew.

One night she came to my bedside
Where I lay fast asleep;
She laid her head upon my bed,
And then began to weep.
She sighed, she cried, she damn near died,
She said – 'What shall I do?' –
So I hauled her into bed and I covered up her head,
Just to save her from the foggy, foggy dew.

Oh, I am a bachelor, I live with my son,
And we work at the weaver's trade;
And every, every time that I look into his eyes,
He reminds me of that maid.
He reminds me of the winter time,
And of the summer, too;
And the many, many times that I held her in my arms,
Just to keep her from the foggy, foggy dew.

THE YOUNG LADY FROM WANTAGE

There was a young lady from Wantage
Of whom the town clerk took advantage.
      Said the borough surveyor:
    'Indeed you must pay 'er.
You've totally altered her frontage.'

THE UNFAITHFUL SHEPHERDESS

While that the sun with his beams hot
Scorched the fruits in vale and mountain,
Philon the shepherd, late forgot,
Sitting beside a crystal fountain,
  In shadow of a green oak tree
  Upon his pipe this song play'd he;
Adieu Love, adieu Love, untrue Love;
Untrue Love, untrue Love, adieu Love;
Your mind is light, soon lost for new love.

So long as I was in your sight
I was your heart, your soul, and treasure;
And evermore you sobb'd and sigh'd
Burning in flames beyond all measure:
  - Three days endured your love to me,
  And it was lost in other three!
Adieu Love, adieu Love, untrue Love;
Untrue Love, untrue Love, adieu Love;
Your mind is light, soon lost for new love.

Another Shepherd you did see
To whom your heart was soon enchained;
Full soon your love was leapt from me,
Full soon my place he had obtained.
  Soon came a third, your love to win,
  And we were out and he was in.
Adieu Love, adieu Love, untrue Love;
Untrue Love, untrue Love, adieu Love;
Your mind is light, soon lost for new love.

Sure you have made me passing glad
That you your mind so soon removed,
Before that I the leisure had
To choose you for my best-beloved:
    For all your love was past and done
    Two days before it was begun.
Adieu Love, adieu Love, untrue Love;
Untrue Love, untrue Love, adieu Love;
Your mind is light, soon lost for new love.

APPLES ON A LILAC TREE

A little boy and a little girl
In an ecstasy of bliss.
Said the little boy to the little girl,
'Pray give me just one kiss.'
The girl drew back in great surprise.
'You're a stranger, sir,' said she.
'But I will give you just one kiss
When the apples grow on the lilac tree.'

The boy was very sad at heart:
She was the only one.
The girl felt quite remorseful
At the terrible wrong she had done.
So very early on the very next morn
He was quite surprised to see
His little sweetheart standing in the garden
Tying apples on the lilac tree!

THE BISHOP'S MISTAKE

The bishop glanced through his window-pane
On a world of sleet, and wind, and rain,
When a dreary figure met his eyes
That made the bishop soliloquize.

And as the bishop gloomily thought
He ordered pen and ink to be brought,
Then 'Providence Watches' he plainly wrote
And pinned the remark to a ten-bob note.

Seizing his hat from his lordly rack
And wrapping his cloak around his back,
Across the road the bishop ran
And gave the note to the shabby man.

That afternoon was the bishop's 'at home'
When everyone gathered beneath his dome,
Curate and canon from far and near
Came to partake of the bishop's cheer.

There in the good old bishop's hall
Stood a stranger lean and tall,
'Your winnings, my lord,' he cried. 'Well done!
'Providence Watches', at ten to one.'

It is to be noted on Sunday next
The bishop skilfully chose his text,
And from the pulpit earnestly told
Of the fertile seed that returned tenfold.

DUST IF YOU MUST

Dust if you must, but wouldn't it be better
To paint a picture or write a letter,
Bake a cake or plant a seed,
Ponder the difference between want and need?

Dust if you must, but there's not much time,
With rivers to swim and mountains to climb,
Music to hear and books to read,
Friends to cherish and life to lead.

Dust if you must, but the world's out there,
With the sun in your eyes, the wind in your hair,
A flutter of snow, a shower of rain.
This day will not come around again.

Dust if you must, but bear in mind,
Old age will come and it's not kind.
And when you go – and go you must –
You, yourself, will make more dust.

I HAD A LITTLE NUT-TREE

I had a little nut-tree,
Nothing would it bear,
But a silver nutmeg,
And a golden pear.
The king of Spain's daughter,
Came to visit me,
And all for the sake,
Of my little nut-tree.

GAELIC BLESSING

Deep peace of the running wave to you.
Deep peace of the flowing air to you.
Deep peace of the quiet earth to you.
Deep peace of the shining stars to you.
Deep peace of the gentle night to you.
Moon and stars pour their healing light on you.
Deep peace of Christ, the light of the world to you.
Deep peace of Christ to you.

FOOTPRINTS

One night I had a dream.
I dreamed I was walking along the
beach with God, and across the sky
flashed scenes from my life. For each
scene I noticed two sets of footprints in
the sand, one belonged to me and the
other to God.

When the last scene of my life flashed
before us I looked back at the footprints
in the sand. I noticed that at times
along the path of life there was only one
set of footprints.
I also noticed that it happened at the
very lowest and saddest times of my
life. This really bothered me and I
questioned God about it.
'God, you said that once I decided to
follow you, you would walk with me all
the way, but I noticed that during the
most troublesome times in my life there
is only one set of footprints. I don't
understand why in times when I needed
you most, you would leave me.'

God replied, 'My precious, precious
child, I love you and would never, never
leave you during your times of trials and
suffering. When you see only one set of
footprints, it was then that I carried you.'

33

GAELIC PRAYER

May the road rise to meet you,
May the wind be always at your back,
May the sun shine warm upon your face,
May the rains fall softly upon your fields.
Until we meet again,
May God hold you in the hollow of his hand.

OLD IRISH TOAST

May you have food and raiment,
A soft pillow for your head.
May you be forty years in heaven
Before the devil knows you're dead.

HERE'S A HEALTH UNTO HER MAJESTY

THE NATIONAL ANTHEM

God save our gracious Queen,
Long live our noble Queen,
　　God save the Queen.
Send her victorious,
Happy and glorious,
Long to reign over us,
　　God save the Queen.

O Lord our God arise,
Scatter our enemies,
　　And make them fall.
Confound their politics,
Frustrate their knavish tricks,
On Thee our hope we fix,
God save us all.

Thy choicest gifts in store,
On her be pleased to pour,
　　Long may she reign.
May she defend our laws,

And ever give us cause,
To sing with heart and voice,
   God save the Queen.

FLAG OF BRITAIN

Flag of Britain proudly waving
Over many distant seas,
Flag of Britain boldly braving
Blinding fog and adverse breeze.
We salute thee and we pray
Bless, oh God, our land today.

Flag of Britain wheresoever
Thy bright colours are outspread,
Slavery must cease forever,
Light and freedom reign instead.
We salute thee and we pray
Bless, oh God, our land today.

Flag of Britain 'mid the nations,
May it ever speak of peace
And proclaim to farthest stations
All unworthy strife must cease.
We salute thee and we pray,
Bless, oh God, our land today.

But if duty sternly need it,
Freely let it be unfurled,
Winds of heaven they may speed it
To each quarter of the world.

We salute thee and we pray,
Bless, oh God, our land today.

Love of it across the waters,
Passing with electric thrill,
Binds our distant sons and daughters
Heart to heart with Britain still.
We salute it and we pray,
Bless, oh God, our land today.

Regions east and west united,
All our Empire knit in one
By right loyal hearts depended
Let it wave beneath the sun.
We salute it and we pray,
Bless, oh God, our land today.

HERE'S A HEALTH UNTO HIS MAJESTY

Here's a health unto his Majesty,
With a fa la la la la la la.
Confusion to his enemies,
With a fa la la la la la la.
And he that will not drink his health!
I wish him neither wit nor wealth,
Nor yet a rope to hang himself!
With a fa la la la la la la la la la!
With a fa la la la la la la la!

All Cavaliers will please combine,
With a fa la la la la la la.
To drink this loyal toast of wine,
With a fa la la la la la la.
If any one should answer 'No',
I only wish that he may go,
With Roundhead rogues to Jericho.
With a fa la la la la la la la la la!
With a fa la la la la la la la!

TO WINSTON CHURCHILL

When half the world was deaf and mute,
  You told of wrath to come,
When others fingered on the lute,
  You thundered on the drum.

When fierce the fires of slaughter burned
  And Europe's hopes were few,
Those who had mocked your warning, turned
  Almost too late to you.

You promised only what you gave –
  As refuge from the flood.
You knew that only you could save
  Through sweat and tears and blood.

Your words upheld our courage yet,
  Through five remorseless years.
You gave us glory in the sweat
  And laughter through the tears.

The storm blew by – the light broke though
  The world returned to form.
Then all our hearts went out to you –
  The man who rode the storm.

In England's cloud-swept history
  Never so great a debt
Was owed by all to one – and we,
  God grant, will not forget.

QUEEN VICTORIA, 1837–1901

Welcome now, VICTORIA!
Welcome to the throne!
May all the trades begin to stir,
    Now you are Queen of England;
For your most gracious Majesty,
May see what wretched poverty,
Is to be found on England's ground,
    Now you are Queen of England.

While o'er the country you preside,
Providence will be your guide,
The people then will never chide
    Victoria, Queen of England.
She doth declare it her intent
To extend reform in Parliament,
On doing good she's firmly bent,
    While she is Queen of England.

Says she, I'll try my utmost skill,
That the poor may have their fill;
Forsake them! – no, I never will,
    When I am Queen of England.
For oft my mother said to me,
Let this your study always be,
To see the people blest and free,
    Should you be Queen of England.

A NEW SONG ON THE BIRTH OF THE PRINCE OF WALES

There's a pretty fuss and bother both in country and
    in town,
Since we have got a present, and an heir unto
    the Crown,
A little Prince of Wales so charming and so sly,
And the ladies shout with wonder, What a pretty
    little boy!

He must have a little musket, a trumpet and a kite,
A little penny rattle, and silver sword so bright,
A little cap and feather with scarlet coat so smart,
And a pretty little hobby-horse to ride about the park.

Prince Albert he will often take the young Prince on
    his lap,
And fondle him so lovingly, while he stirs about the pap,
He will pin on his flannel before he takes his nap,
Then dress him out so stylish with his little clouts
    and cap.

He must have a dandy suit to strut about the town,
John Bull must rake together six or seven
    thousand pound,
You'd laugh to see his daddy, at night he
    homeward runs,
With some peppermint or lollipops, sweet cakes
    and sugar plums.

He will want a little fiddle, and a little German flute,
A little pair of stockings and a pretty pair of boots,
With a handsome pair of spurs, and a golden-
    headed cane,
And a stick of barley sugar, as long as Drury Lane.

An old maid ran through the palace, which did the
    nobs surprise,
Bawling out, he's got his daddy's mouth, his mammy's
    nose and eyes,
He will be as like his daddy as a frigate to a ship,
If he'd only got mustachios upon his upper lip.

Now to get these little niceties the taxes must be rose,
For the little Prince of Wales wants so many suits
    of clothes,
So they must tax the frying pan, the windows and
    the doors,
The bedsteads and the tables, kitchen pokers, and
    the floors.

KING ALFRED AND THE CAKES

Where lying on the hearth to bake
By chance the cake did burn:
'What! Canst thou not, thou lout,' quoth she,
'Take pains the same to turn?
But serve me such another trick,
I'll thwack thee on the snout.'
Which made the patient, kind, good man,
Of her to stand in doubt.

PRINCE ALBERT

I am a German just arrived,
    With you for to be mingling,
My passage it was paid,
    From Germany to England;
To wed your blooming Queen.
    For better or worse I take her,
My father is a duke,
    And I'm a sausage-maker.

        Here I am in rags and jags,
        Come from the land of all dirt,
        I married England's Queen.
        My name it is young Albert.

I am a cousin to the Queen,
    And our mothers they are cronies,
My father lives at home,
    And deals in nice polonies:
Lots of sour crout and broom,
    For money he'll be giving,
And by working very hard,
    He gets a tidy living.

        Here I am, &c.

She says now we are wed,
    I must not dare to tease her,

But strive both day and night,
    All e'er I can to please her,
I told her I would do
    For her all I was able,
And when she had a son
    I would sit and rock the cradle.

    Here I am, &c.

LOVE & MARRIAGE

WHAT IS LOVE?

LOVE IS not just looking at each other and saying
    'You're wonderful'.
There are times when we are anything but wonderful.
Love is looking out in the same direction. It is linking
    our strength to pull a common load. It is pushing
    together towards the far horizons, hand in hand.
Love is knowing that when our strength falters, we
    can borrow the strength of someone who cares.
Love is a strange awareness that our sorrows will be
    shared and made lighter by sharing; that joys will
    be enriched and multiplied by the joy of another.
Love is knowing someone else cares that we are not
    alone in life.

LOVE IS GIVING

Love is giving, not taking,
mending, not breaking,
trusting, believing,
never deceiving,
patiently bearing
and faithfully sharing
each joy, every sorrow.
Today and tomorrow.

Love is kind, understanding,
but never demanding.
Love is constant, prevailing,
its strength never failing.
A promise once spoken
for all time unbroken,
a lifetime together,
love's time is for ever.

A GOOD WEDDING CAKE

4 lb of love
$^{1}/_{2}$ old of good looks
1 lb of butter of youth
1 lb of blindness of faults
1 lb of self-forgetfulness
1 lb of pounded wit
1 lb of good humour
2 tablespoons of sweet argument
1 pint of rippling laughter
1 wine glass of common sense
1 oz of modesty

Put the love, good looks and sweet temper into a well-furnished house. Beat the butter of youth to a cream, and mix well together with the blindness of faults and self-forgetfulness. Stir the pounded wit and good humour into the sweet argument, then add the rippling laughter, common sense and modesty. Work the whole together until everything is well mixed, and bake gently forever.

FAIR HELEN

I wish I were where Helen lies;
Night and day on me she cries;
O that I were where Helen lies
    On fair Kirconnell lea!

Curst be the heart that thought the thought,
And curst the hand that fired the shot,
When in my arms burd Helen dropt,
    And died to succour me!

O think na but my heart was sair
When my Love dropt down and spak nae mair!
I laid her down wi' meikle care
    On fair Kirconnell lea.

As I went down the water-side,
None but my foe to be my guide,
None but my foe to be my guide,
    On fair Kirconnell lea;

I lighted down my sword to draw,
I hacked him in pieces sma',
I hacked him in pieces sma'
    For her sake that died for me.

O Helen fair, beyond compare!
I'll make a garland of thy hair
Shall bind my heart for evermair
    Until the day I die.

O that I were where Helen lies!
Night and day on me she cries;
Out of my bed she bids me rise,
    Says, 'Haste and come to me!'

O Helen fair! O Helen chaste!
If I were with thee I were blest,
Where thou lies low and takes thy rest
    On fair Kirconnell lea.

I wish my grave were growing green,
A winding-sheet drawn ower my een,
And I in Helen's arms lying,
    On fair Kirconnell lea.

I wish I were where Helen lies;
Night and day on me she cries;
And I am weary of the skies,
    Since my love died for me.

THESE I CAN PROMISE

I cannot promise you a life of sunshine;
I cannot promise riches, wealth, or gold;
I cannot promise you an easy pathway
That leads away from change or growing old.

But I can promise all my heart's devotion;
A smile to chase away your tears of sorrow;
A love that's ever true and ever-growing;
A hand to hold in yours through each tomorrow.

APACHE BLESSING

May the sun bring you new energy by day,
May the moon softly restore you by night,
May the rain wash away your worries
And the breeze blow new strength into your being,
And all of the days of your life may you walk
Gently through the world and know its beauty.

THE PLACE

The place whence comes each happy inspiration …
Where love serenely dwells … and hope is born …
Where strivings cease … and strife is barred the door.
Where confidence is bred … and the eloquence of
    silence understood.
A place where plans are made and journeys start,
Where journeys end in happy welcomings.

Where dwells that peace so eagerly desired by all …
And mutual trust survives whate'er befall.
Where laughter is not very far away, and truth
    is reverenced.
Where friends drop in to share our joys or woes,
And absent friends are ever in our thoughts.
God give you such a home.

AMERICAN INDIAN WEDDING BLESSING

Now you will feel no rain,
>for each of you will be shelter to the other.

Now you will feel no cold,
>for each of you will be warmth to the other.

Now you will feel no loneliness,
>for each of you will be companionship to the other.

Now you are two persons,
>but there are three lives before you: his life, her
>life and your life together.

Go now to your dwelling place,
>to enter into the days of your life together.

May beauty surround you both in the journey ahead
>and through all the years may happiness be
>your companion,

And may your days be good and long upon the earth.

Treat yourselves and each other with respect,
>And remind yourselves often of what brought
>you together.

Give the highest priority to the tenderness, gentleness
>and kindness that your connection deserves.

When frustration, difficulty and fear assail your
>relationship,remember to focus on what is right
>between you, not only that part which seems wrong.

In this way, you can ride out the storms
>when clouds hide the face of the sun in your lives.

THIS DAY I MARRIED MY BEST FRIEND

This day I married my best friend
    ... the one I laugh with as we share life's
    wondrous zest,
as we find new enjoyments and experience all
    that's best.
... the one I live for because the world seems brighter
as our happy times are better and our burdens
    feel much lighter.
... the one I love with every fibre of my soul.
We used to feel vaguely incomplete, now together
    we are whole.

LOVE DOES NOT CONSIST IN GAZING AT ONE ANOTHER

Love does not consist in gazing at one another,
But in looking outward together in the same direction.
Do not seek perfection in each other.
Do not seek to make the other into your own image,
or to remake yourself into another's image.
What each most truly is will be known by the other.
It is that truth of you which must be loved.
Many things will change, but change is not the
    enemy of love.
Change is the enemy only of any attempt to possess.
May all that is good and true and beautiful
Abide with you now and always.

HINDU MARRIAGE POEM

You have become mine forever.
Yes, we have become partners.
I have become yours.
Hereafter, I cannot live without you.
Do not live without me.
Let us share the joys.
We are word and meaning, unite.
You are thought and I am sound.
May the nights be honey-sweet for us.
May the mornings be honey-sweet for us.
May the plants be honey-sweet for us.
May the earth be honey-sweet for us.

A WALLED GARDEN

'Your marriage,' he said, 'should have within it, a
    secret and protected place open to you alone.
'Imagine it to be a walled garden, entered by a door
    to which you only hold the key.
'Within this garden you will cease to be a mother,
    father, employee, homemaker or any other of the
    roles which you fulfil in daily life.
'Here you are yourselves – two people, who love
    each other.
'Here you can concentrate on one another's needs.'
And so we made our walled garden.
Time that was kept for us alone.
At first we went there often, enjoying each other's
    company, sharing secrets, growing closer.
But now our days are packed with plans and people.
Conversation has become a message scribbled on a pad.
The door into our garden is almost hidden by rank
    weeds of busy-ness.
We claim we have no time because we have forgotten.
Forgotten that love grows if it is tended, and if
    neglected, dies.
But we can always make the time for what is most
    important in our lives.
So take my hand and let us go back to our garden.
The time we spend together is not wasted but invested,
Invested in our future and the nurture of our love.

THE MAIDEN'S LAMENT

ONE morning very early, one morning in the spring,
I heard a maid in Bedlam who mournfully did sing,
Her chains she rattled on her hands while sweetly
    thus sung she,
I love my love, because I know my love loves me.

Oh cruel were his parents who sent my love to sea,
And cruel, cruel was the ship that bore my love from me,
Yet I love his parents since they're his, although
    they've ruined me,
And I love my love, because I know my love loves me.

Oh should it please the pitying powers to call me to
    the sky,
I'd claim a guardian angel's charge around my love
    to fly;
To guard him from all dangers how happy should I be!
For I love my love, because I know my love loves me.

I'll make a strawy garland, I'll make it wondrous fine,
With roses, lilies, daisies, I'll mix the eglantine;
And I'll present it to my love when he returns from sea,
For I love my love, because I know my love loves me.

Oh if I were a little bird to build upon his breast,
Or if I were a nightingale to sing my love to rest!
To gaze upon his lovely eyes all my reward should be;
For I love my love, because I know my love loves me.

Oh if I were an eagle, to soar into the sky!
I'd gaze around with piercing eyes where I my love
        might spy;
But ah! unhappy maiden, that love you ne'er shall see,
Yet I love my love, because I know my love loves me.

ON YOUR WEDDING DAY

Today is a day you will always remember
        The greatest in anyone's life.
You'll start off the day just two people in love
        And end it as Husband and Wife.
It's a brand-new beginning, the start of a journey
        With moments to cherish and treasure
And although there'll be times when you both disagree
        These will surely be outweighed by pleasure.
You'll have heard many words of advice in the past
        When the secrets of marriage were spoken
But you know that the answers lie hidden inside
        Where the bond of true love lies unbroken.
So live happy forever as lovers and friends
        It's the dawn of a new life for you
As you stand there together with love in your eyes
        For the moment you whisper 'I do'.
And with luck, all your hopes, and your dreams can
        be real.
        May success find its way to your hearts.
Tomorrow can bring you the greatest of joys,
        But today is the day it all starts.

O, WHO WILL O'ER THE DOWNS

O, who will o'er the downs so free,
O, who will with me ride,
O, who will up and follow me,
To win a blooming bride?
Her father he has locked the door,
Her mother keeps the key,
But neither door nor bolt shall part
My own true love from me.

I saw her bower at twilight grey,
'Twas guarded safe and sure,
I saw her bower at break of day,
'Twas guarded then no more.
The varlets they were all asleep,
And none was there to see
The greeting fair that passed there
Between my love and me.

And promised her to come at night
With comrades brave and true,
A gallant band with sword in hand,
To break her prison through.
I promised her to come at night,
She's waiting now for me,
And ere the dawn of morning light
I'll set my true love free,
And ere the dawn of morning light
I'll set my true love free.

THE HAPPINESS OF THE WORLD

To have a cheerful, bright, and airy dwelling place
With garden, lawns, and climbing flowers sweet;
Fresh fruits, good wine, few children; there to meet
A quiet, faithful wife, whose love shines through
　　her face.

To have no debt, no lawyer's feud' no love but one,
And not too much to do with one's relations.
Be just, and be content. Nought but vexations
Arise from toadying the great, when all is done.

Live well and wisely, and for grate petition;
Indulge devotion to its full fruition;
Subdue your passions – that is the best condition.
Your mind untrammelled, and your heart in Faith;
While at your business give your prayers breath;
This is to rest at home, and calmly wait for death.

A REVERSIBLE LOVE POEM

These verses may be read, line by line, either up or down without altering the sense.

The stars were all alight,
    The moon was overhead;
I named her queen of night,
    And she my footsteps led.
So wondrous fair was she,
    I asked her to be mine.
As she glanced up at me
    I thrilled with love divine.

Beside the meadow bars,
    As she stood lingering there,
Her eyes were like the stars,
    In radiance wondrous fair.
'You're all the world to me,'
    She murmured sweet and shy.
A thrill of ecstasy
    I felt at her reply.

Love led us all the way,
    As we turned home again;
Our hearts were light and gay,
    The world was blissful then,
Though shadows cross the sky,
    No gloom our hearts could know;
True bliss is ever nigh
    When hearts are blended so.

SUSAN SIMPSON

Sudden swallows swiftly skimming,
    Sunset's slowly spreading shade,
Silvery songsters sweetly singing
    Summer's soothing serenade.

Susan Simpson strolled sedately,
    Stifling sobs, suppressing sighs.
Seeing Stephen Slocum, stately
    She stopped, showing some surprise.

'Say,' said Stephen, 'sweetest sigher;
    Say, shall Stephen spouseless stay?'
Susan, seeming somewhat shyer,
    Showed submissiveness straightaway.

Summer's season slowly stretches,
    Susan Simpson Slocum she –
So she signed some simple sketches –
    Soul sought soul successfully.

Six Septembers Susan swelters;
    Six sharp seasons snow supplied;
Susan's satin sofa shelters
    Six small Slocums side by side.

GREENSLEEVES

Alas! my love, you do me wrong
To cast me off discourteously;

and I have loved you so long,
Delighting in your company.

Greensleeves was all my joy!
Greensleeves was my delight!
Greensleeves was my heart of gold!
And who but my Lady Greensleeves!

I bought thee petticoats of the best,
The cloth so fine as fine as might be;
I gave thee jewels for thy chest,
And all this cost I spent on thee.

Thy smock of silk, both fair and white,
With gold embroidered gorgeously;
Thy petticoat of sendal right:
And these I bought thee gladly.

Thy gown was of the grassy green,
The sleeves of satin hanging by;
Which made thee be our harvest queen:
And yet thou wouldest not love me!

Greensleeves now farewell! adieu!
God I pray to prosper thee!
For I am still thy lover true:
Come once again and love me!

Greensleeves was all my joy!
Greensleeves was my delight!
Greensleeves was my heart of gold!
And who but my Lady Greensleeves!

WHO PLUCKED THIS FLOWER?

This beautiful epitaph on a child's gravestone
occurs in Sellack Churchyard, Herefordshire, and in
other forms elsewhere.

The gardener asked, 'Who plucked this
flower?
The Master said, 'I plucked it for Myself,'
and the gardener held his peace.

LONDON TOWN

CHRISTOPHER WREN

Clever men like Christopher Wren
Only occur just now and then.
No one expects in perpetuity
Architects of his ingenuity;
No, never a cleverer dipped his pen
Than clever Sir Christopher, Christopher Wren.
With his chaste designs on classical lines
His elegant curves and neat inclines
Every day of the week was filled
With a church to mend or a church to build,
And never an hour goes by but when
London needed Sir Christopher Wren.
'Brides' in Fleet Street lacks a spire,
'Mary-le-Bow' a nave and choir.
'Please to send the plans complete,
For a new St Stephens, Coleman Street.'
'Pewterer's Hall is far too tall,
'Kindly lower the North West wall.'
'Salisbury Square decidedly bare,
'Can you put one of your churches there?'

'Dome of St Paul's is not yet done,
Dean's been waiting since half-past one.'
London calling from ten till ten,
London calling Sir Christopher Wren.

LONDON BRIDGE IS FALLING DOWN

London Bridge is falling down,
Falling down, falling down,
London Bridge is falling down,
My fair Lady.

Build it up with wood and clay,
Wood and clay, wood and clay,
Build it up with wood and clay
My fair Lady.

Wood and clay will wash away,
Wash away, wash away,
Wood and clay will wash away,
My fair Lady.

Build it up with bricks and mortar,
Bricks and mortar, bricks and mortar,
Build it up with bricks and mortar,
My fair Lady.

Bricks and mortar will not stay,
Will not stay, will not stay,
Bricks and mortar will not stay,
My fair Lady.

Build it up with iron and steel,
Iron and steel, iron and steel,
Build it up with iron and steel,
My fair Lady.

Iron and steel will bend and bow,
Bend and bow, bend and bow,
Iron and steel will bend and bow,
My fair Lady.

Build it up with silver and gold,
Silver and gold, silver and gold,
Build it up with silver and gold,
My fair Lady.

Silver and gold will be stolen away,
Stolen away, stolen away,
Silver and gold will be stolen away,
My fair Lady.

Set a man to watch all night,
Watch all night, watch all night,
Set a man to watch all night,
My fair Lady.

Suppose the man should fall asleep?
Fall asleep, fall asleep,
Suppose the man should fall asleep?
My fair Lady.

Give him a pipe to smoke all night,
Smoke all night, smoke all night,
Give him a pipe to smoke all night,
My fair Lady.

THE GREAT EXHIBITION

Fountains, gushing silver light,
    Sculptures, soft and warm and fair,
Gems, that blind the dazzled sight,
    Silken trophies rich and rare,
Wondrous works of cunning skill,
    Precious miracles of art,
How your crowding memories fill
    Mournfully my musing heart!

Fairy Giant choicest birth
    Of the Beautiful Sublime,
Seeming like the Toy of earth
    Given to the dotard Time,
Glacier-diamond, Alp of glass,
    Sinbad's cave, Aladdin's hall,
Must it then be crush'd, alas;
    Must the Crystal Palace fall?

LONDON MOURNING IN ASHES

Of Fire, Fire, Fire I sing,
    that have more cause to cry,
In the Great Chamber of the King,
    (a City mounted High;)
Old London that,
Hath stood in State,
    above six hundred years,
In six days space,

Woe and alas!
    is burn'd and drown'd in tears.

The second of September in
    the middle time of night,
In Pudding Lane it did begin,
    to burn and blaze outright;
Where all that gaz'd,
Were so amaz'd
    at such a furious flame,
They knew not how,
Or what to do
    that might expel the same.

It swallow'd Fishstreet Hil, & straight
    it lick'd up Lombard Street,
Down Canon Street in blazing state
    it flew with flaming feet;
Down to the Thames
Whose shrinking streams,
    began to ebb away,
As thinking that,
The power of Fate
    had brought the latter day ...

IF I WERE KING

If I were King George of England,
    I would take one day
The oldest coat that could be found,
    And I would run away.

I'd quickly hurry down the stairs
    When no one was about,
And past my sentries at the gate
    I'd hurry quickly out.

I'd pull my hat down very tight,
    And glasses on my nose,
Would wander into Regent Street
    Where everybody goes.

I'd stand outside the crowded shops
    And gaze at everything
And not a single soul I met would
    Know I was the king.

I'd get a passing omnibus to take
    Me to the Strand.
And hail the bus conductor by just
    holding up my hand.

He wouldn't say 'Your Majesty'
    If I went for a ride,
But 'hurry up' – and – 'Pass along!'
    And 'Room for one inside.'

And – 'Two pence please!' – and
    'Mind the step.' How funny it would be
To see my London – just for once
    Without it seeing me!

LONDON BELLS

Two sticks and an apple,
Ring the bells at Whitechapel.

Old Father Bald Pate,
Ring the bells of Aldgate.

Maids in white aprons,
Ring the bells at St Catherine's.

Oranges and lemons,
Ring the bells at St Clement's.

When will you pay me?
Ring the bells of Old Bailey.

When I am rich,
Ring the bells at Fleetditch.

When will that be?
Ring the bells at Stepney.

When I am old,
Rings the great bell at Paul's.

A SONNET UPON THE PITIFUL BURNING OF
THE GLOBE PLAYHOUSE IN LONDON

Now sitt thee downe, Melpomene,
Wrapt in a sea-coal robe,
And tell the dolefull tragedie,
That late was play'd at Globe;
For noe man that can singe and saye
But was scar'd on St Peter's Daye.
Oh sorrow, pittifull sorrow, and yet all this is true.

All yow that please to understand,
Come listen to my storye,
To see Death with his rakeing brand
'Mongst such an auditorye;
Regarding neither Cardinalls might,
Nor yet the rugged face of Henry the Eight.
Oh sorrow, pittifull sorrow, and yet all this is true.

This fearfull fire beganne above,
A wonder strange and true,
And to the stage-howse did remove,
As round as tailors clewe;
And burnt downe both beame and snagg,
And did not spare the silken flagg.
Oh sorrow, pitiful sorrow, and yet all this is true.

Out runne the knightes, out runne the lordes,
And there was great adoe;
Some lost their hates and some their swords;
Then out runne Burbidge too;
The reprobates, though druncke on Munday,
Pray'd for the Foole and Henry Condye.
Oh sorrow, pittifull sorrow, and yet all this is true.

The perrywigges and drumme-heades frye,
Like to a butter firkin;
A woefull burneing did betide
To many a good buffe jerkin.
Then with swolne eyes, like druncken Flemminges,
Distressed stood old stuttering Heminges.
Oh sorrow, pittifull sorrow, and yet all this is true.

No shower his raine did there downe force
In all that Sunn-shine weather,
To save that great renowned howse;
Nor thou, O ale-howse, neither.
Had itt begunne belowe, sans doubte,
Their wives for feare had pissed itt out.
Oh sorrow, pittifull sorrow, and yet all this is true.

Bee warned, yow stage strutters all,
Least yow againe be catched,
And such a burneing doe befall,
As to them whose howse was thatched;
Forbeare your whoreing, breeding biles,
And laye up that expence for tiles.
Oh sorrow, pittifull sorrow, and yet all this is true.

Goe drawe yow a petition,
And dow yow not abhor itt,
And gett, with low submission,
A licence to begg for itt
In churches, sans churchwardens checkes,
In Surrey and Middlesex,
Oh sorrow, pittifull sorrow, and yet all this is true.

HERE'S THE MAN A-COMING!

In Lunnon town each day, strange sayings will
    be springing,
But, if you list to me, a new one I'll be singing,
As you go through the town, the people will be funning,
One cries out, 'Put it down, here's the man a-coming!'

'Twas only t'other day, as sure as I'm a sinner,
A leg of pork I bought, to have a slap-up dinner;
When, halfway down the street, a young scamp came
    by, running,
Says he, 'Guvner, drop that meat, here's the
    man a-coming!'

Young married folks, I fear, to extremes often dash on,
They're always in a fright, through studying the fashion;
Each day with fear and dread, the tradesmen they
    are shunning,
'Jem, get under the bed, here's the tally man a-coming!'

There's lots of ups and downs, and lots of
    rummy dodgings,
But I do it quite brown, in taking furnish'd lodgings;
I own I'm very poor, to pay there is no fun in,
So I always bolt the door when I hear the
    landlord coming!
It's pleasant, in this place, to see your smiling faces.
And, gents, too, I presume, you're in your proper places;
Now, there's one stands there so sly, I know he's
    very cunning,
I say, 'Mind what you're at, here's the man a-coming!'

THE CRIES OF LONDON

Here's fine rosemary, sage, and thyme
Come buy my ground ivy.
Here's fetherfew, gillyflowers and rue.
Come buy my knotted marjorum, ho!
Come buy my mint, my fine green mint.
Here's fine lavender for your cloaths.
Here's parsley and winter-savory,
And hearts-ease, which all do choose.
Here's balm and hyssop, and cinquefoil,
All fine herbs, it is well known.
    Let none despise the merry, merry cries
    Of famous London-town!

Here's fine herrings, eight a groat.
Hot codlins, pies and tarts.
New mackerel! have to sell.
Come buy my Wellfleet oysters, ho!
Come buy my whitings fine and new.
Wives, shall I mend your husband's horns?
I'll grind your knives to please your wives,
And very nicely cut your corns.
Maids, have you any hair to sell,
Either flaxen, black, or brown?
    Let none despise the merry, merry cries
    Of famous London-town!

WOT CHER!
OR, KNOCKED 'EM IN THE OLD KENT ROAD

Last week down our alley came a toff,
Nice old geezer with a nasty cough,
Sees my Missus, takes 'is topper off
    In a very gentlemanly way!
'Ma'am,' says he, 'I 'ave some news to tell,
Your rich Uncle Tom of Camberwell
Popped off recent, which it ain't a sell,
Leaving you 'is little Donkey Shay.'

    'Wot cher!' all the neighbours cried,
        'Who're yer goin' to meet, Bill?
        Have yer bought the street, Bill?
    Laugh! I thought I should 'ave died,
    Knocked 'em in the Old Kent Road!

Some says nasty things about the moke,
One cove thinks 'is leg is really broke,
That's 'is envy, cos we're carriage folk,
    Like the Toffs as rides in Rotten Row!
Straight! it woke the alley up a bit,
Thought our lodger would 'ave 'ad a fit,
When my misses, who's a real wit,
    Says, 'I 'ates a Bus, because it's low!'

    'Wot cher!' all the neighbours cried,
        'Who're yer goin' to meet, Bill?
        Have yer bought the street, Bill?
    Laugh! I thought I should 'ave died,
    Knocked 'em in the Old Kent Road!

When we starts the blessed donkey stops,
He won't move, so out I quickly 'ops,
Pals start whackin' him when down he drops,
    Someone says he wasn't made to go.
Lor, it might have been a four-in-'and,
My Old Dutch knows 'ow to do the grand,
First she bows, and then she waves 'er 'and,
    Calling out we're goin' for a blow!

    'Wot cher!' all the neighbours cried,
       'Who're yer goin' to meet, Bill?
       Have yer bought the street, Bill?
    Laugh! I thought I should 'ave died,
    Knocked 'em in the Old Kent Road!

Ev'ry evenin' on the stroke of five
Me and Missus takes a little drive,
You'd say, 'Wonderful they're still alive,'
    If you saw that little donkey go.
I soon showed him that 'e'd have to do
Just whatever he was wanted to,
Still I shan't forget that rowdy crew,
    'Ollerin', 'Woa! steady! Neddy woa!'

    'Wot cher!' all the neighbours cried,
       'Who're yer goin' to meet, Bill?
       Have yer bought the street, Bill?
    Laugh! I thought I should 'ave died,
    Knocked 'em in the Old Kent Road!

THE MAID'S LONGING

A maiden of late
Whose name was Sweet Kate,
She dwelt in London near Aldersgate;
    Now list to my ditty, declare it I can,
    She wuld have a child without help of a man.

To a doctor she came,
A man of great fame,
Whose deep skill in physick report did proclaim.
    Quoth she: 'Mr Doctor, shew me if you can
    How I may conceive without help of a man.'

'Then listen,' quoth he,
'Since it must be,
This wondrous strange med'cine I'll shew presently;
    Take nine pound of thunder, six legs of a swan,
    And you shall conceive without help of a man.

'The love of false harlots,
The faith of false varlets,
With the truth of decoys that walk in their scarlet,
    And the feathers of a lobster, well fry'd in a pan,
    And you shall conceive without help of a man.

'Nine drops of rain
Brought hither from Spain,
With the blast of a bellows quite over the main,
    With eight quarts of brimstone brew'd in a can,
    And you shall conceive without help of a man.

'Six pottles of lard,
Squeez'd from rock hard,
With nine turkey eggs, each as long as a yard,
     With pudding of hailstones well bak'd in a pan,
     And you shall conceive without help of a man.

'These med'cines are good,
And approved have stood,
Well temper'd together with a pottle of blood
     Squeez'd from a grasshopper and the nail of a swan,
     To make maids conceive without help of a man.'

ANIMAL CRACKERS

THE FROG

What a wonderful bird the frog are!
When he stand he sit almost;
When he hop he fly almost.
He ain't got no sense hardly;
He ain't got no tail hardly either.
When he sit, he sit on what he ain't got almost.

THE IRISH PIG

'Twas an evening in November,
As I very well remember,
I was strolling down the street in drunken pride,
But my knees were all a'flutter
So I landed in the gutter,
And a pig came up and lay down by my side.

Yes, I lay there in the gutter
Thinking thoughts I could not utter,
When a colleen passing by did softly say,
'Ye can tell a man that boozes
By the company he chooses,' –
At that, the pig got up and walked away!

POOR BEASTS!

The horse and mule live thirty years
And nothing know of wines and beers.
The goat and sheep at twenty die
And never taste of Scotch or Rye.
The cow drinks water by the ton
And at eighteen is mostly done.
The dog at fifteen cashes in
Without the aid of rum and gin.
The cat in milk and water soaks
And then in twelve short years it croaks.
The modest, sober, bone-dry hen
Lays eggs for nogs, then dies at ten.
All animals are strictly dry:
They sinless live and swiftly die;
But sinful, ginful, rum-soaked men
Survive for three score years and ten.
And some of them, a very few,
Stay pickled till they're ninety-two.

THE COW

Come, children, listen to me now,
And you shall hear about the cow;
You'll find her useful, alive or dead,
Whether she's black, or white, or red.
When milk-maids milk her, morn or night,
She gives us milk so fresh and white;
And this, we little children think,
Is very nice for us to drink.

The curdled milk they press and squeeze,
And so they make it into cheese;
The cream they skim, and shake in churns,
And then it soon to butter turns.
And when she's dead, her flesh is good,
For beef is our true English food;
But though in health it makes us strong,
To eat too much is very wrong.

Then lime and bark the tanner takes,
And of her skin he leather makes;
And this we know they mostly use
To make us good strong boots and shoes;
And last of all, if cut with care,
Her horns make combs to comb our hair.
And so we learn, thanks to our teachers,
That cows are very useful creatures.

O'RAFFERTY'S PIG

O'Rafferty's pig was a wonderful animal,
Built like a battleship, solid and stout;
His ignorance would have disgraced any cannibal,
Impertinence written all over his snout.

The night he broke loose there was such a commotion,
The women were screaming and the men turning pale,
Colliding and bumping and running and jumping,
And everyone making a grab at its tail.

O'Rafferty got the oul' pig in a corner,
He jumped on its back and ran into a dray,
And at twenty past seven his home was in heaven,
The night that O'Rafferty's pig ran away.

The fat Mrs Doylie she ran like an elephant,
Puffing and blowing with Mrs McGuire;
She fell on the ground and, begorrah! the sound,
Was just like the burst of a pneumatic tyre.

The widow Malone fell through a shop window,
In pickles and jam and red herrings she lay'
She had eggs and tomatoes all over her garters,
The night that O'Rafferty's pig ran away.

Then Paddy McKnoll, the heavy-weight champion,
Ran at the pig with a big rolling-pin,
Struck it a blow which caught Mrs Munroe,
And shifted her bustle right under her chin.

It ran through the legs of old Councillor Duffey,
A man of great standing and lofty ideas;
The pig it collided and Duffey back-slided,
And down went the standing of sixty-five years.

O'Rourke's wooden leg was all shattered and broken,
He lay on the ground calling Doctor Lamont,
Then Barney O'Toole said, 'Don't be a fool,
It's a hammer and saw and a joiner you want!'

It ran through the police-court, looked at each visitor,
Swallowed the Bible, and judge in full rig.
'We will postpone the case' said the local solicitor,
'And just let the witnesses all kiss the pig.'

The pig looked at Reilly, the principal witness,
Then dashed through the grocer's shop, next door
    to McCann's,
He splashed through the butter and then through
    the gutter,
And that's how he kept slipping out of their hands.

At last came the news that the pig has been captured,
They all had a thanks-giving supper they say,
On cabbage and bacon unlawfully taken,
The night that O'Rafferty's pig ran away.

THE MOUSE, THE FROG AND
THE LITTLE RED HEN

Once a Mouse, a Frog, and a Little Red Hen,
Together kept a house;
The Frog was the laziest of frogs,
And lazier still was the Mouse.

The work all fell on the Little Red Hen,
Who had to get the wood,
And build the fires and scrub, and cook,
And sometimes hunt the food.

One day, as she went scratching round,
She found a bag of rye;
Said she, 'Now who will make some bread?'
Said the lazy Mouse, 'Not I.'

'Nor I,' croaked the Frog as he drowsed in the shade,
Red Hen made no replay,
But flew around with bowl and spoon,
And mixed and stirred the rye.

'Who'll make the fire to bake the bread?'
Said the Mouse again. 'Not I,'
And, scarcely op'ning his sleepy eyes,
Frog made the same reply.

The Little Red Hen said never a word,
But a roaring fire she made;
And while the bread was baking brown,
'Who'll set the table?' she said.

'Not I,' said the sleepy Frog with a yawn;
'Nor I,' said the Mouse again.
So the table she set and the bread put on,
'Who'll eat this bread?' said the Hen.

'I will!' cried the Frog. 'And I!' squeaked the Mouse,
As they near the table drew;
'Oh, no, you won't!' said the Little Red Hen,
And away with the loaf she flew.

THE SOW CAME IN

THE SOW came in with the saddle,
The little pig rocked the cradle,
The dish jumped up on the table,
To see the pot swallow the ladle.
The spit that stood behind the door
Called the dish-clout dirty whore.
    Odd's-bob! says the gridiron,
        Can't you agree?
    I'm the head constable,
        Bring them to me.

THE BLEED'N' SPARRER

We 'ad a bleed'n' sparrer wot
Lived up a bleed'n' spaht,
One day the bleed'n' rain came dahn
An' washed the bleeder aht.

An' as 'e layed 'arf drahnded
Dahn in the bleed'n' street
'E begged that bleed'n' rainstorm
To bave 'is bleed'n' feet.

But then the bleed'n' sun came aht –
Dried up the bleed'n' rain –
So that bleed'n' little sparrer
'E climbed up 'is spaht again.

But, Oh! – the crewel sparrer'awk,
'E spies 'im in 'is snuggery,
'E sharpens up 'is bleed'n' claws
An' rips 'im aht by thuggery!

Jist then a bleed'n' sportin' type
Wot 'ad a bleed'n' gun
'E spots that bleed'n' sparrer'awk
An' blasts 'is bleed'n' fun.

The moral of this story
Is plain to everyone –
That them wot's up the bleed'n' spaht
Don't get no bleed'n' fun.

THE AULD SECEDER CAT

There was a Presbyterian cat
Went forth to catch her prey;
She brought a mouse into the house,
Upon the Sabbath day.
The minister, offended
With such an act profane,
Laid down his book, the cat he took,
And bound her with a chain.

Thou vile, malicious creature,
Thou murderer, said he,
Oh do you think to bring to Hell
My hold wife and me?
But be thou well assured,
That blood for blood shall pay,
For taking of the mouse's life
Upon the Sabbath Day.

Then he took doun his Bible,
And fervently he prayed,
That the great sin the cat had done
Might not on him be laid.
Then forth to exe-cu-ti-on,
Poor Baudrons she was drawn,
And on a tree they hanged her hie,
And then they sung a psalm.

NO WONDER HE WAGS HIS TAIL!

When God had made the earth and sky
    The flowers and the trees,
He then made all the animals
    And all the birds and bees.
And when His work was finished
    Not one was quite the same.
He said 'I'll walk this earth of mine
    And give each one a name.'
And so He travelled land and sea
    And everywhere He went
A little creature followed Him
    Until its strength was spent.
When all were named upon the earth
    And in the sky and sea,
The little creature said, 'Dear Lord,
    There's not one left for me.'
The Father smiled and softly said,
    'I've left you to the end.
I've turned my own name back to front
    And called you Dog, my friend.'

THE DEATH AND BURIAL OF POOR COCK ROBIN

Who killed Cock Robin?
'I,' said the Sparrow,
'With my bow and arrow,
I killed Cock Robin.'

Who saw him die?
'I,' said the Fly,
'With my little eye,
I saw him die.'

Who caught his blood?
'I,' said the Fish,
'With my little dish,
I caught his blood.'

Who'll make his shroud?
'I,' said the Beetle,
'With my thread and needle,
I'll make his shroud.'

Who'll dig his grave?
'I,' said the Owl,
'With my spade and trowel,
I'll dig his grave.'

Who'll be the Parson?
'I,' said the Rook,
'With my little book,
I'll be the Parson.'

Who'll be the Clerk?

'I,' said the Lark,
'I'll say Amen in the dark,
I'll be the Clerk.'

Who'll carry the coffin?
'I,' said the Kite,
'If it be in the night,
I'll carry the coffin.'

Who'll bear the torch?
'I,' said the Linnet,
'Will come in a minute,
I'll bear the torch.'

Who'll be chief mourner?
'I,' said the Dove
'I mourn for my love,
I'll be chief mourner.'

Who'll sing a psalm?
'I,' said the Thrush
As she sat in a bush,
'I'll sing a psalm.'

Who'll toll the bell?
'I,' said the Bull,
'Because I can pull,
I'll toll the bell.'

All the birds of the air
Fell sighing and sobbing
When they heard the bell toll
For Poor Cock Robin.

THE COMMON CORMORANT

The common cormorant or shag
Lays eggs inside a paper bag.
The reason you will see, no doubt,
It is to keep the lightning out.
But what these unobservant birds
Have never noticed is that herds
Of wandering bears may come with buns
And steal the bags to hold the crumbs.

LINES BY A HUMANITARIAN

Be lenient with lobsters, and ever kind to crabs,
And be not disrespectful to cuttle-fish or dabs;
Chase not the Cochin-China, chaff not the ox obese,
And babble not of feather-beds in company with geese.
Be tender with the tadpole, and let the limpet thrive,
Be merciful to mussels, don't skin your eels alive;
When talking to a turtle don't mention calipee –
Be always kind to animals wherever you may be.

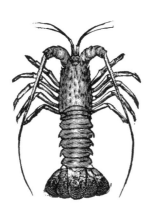

I SAW A FISHPOND

I saw a fishpond all on fire
I saw a house bow to a squire
I saw a parson twelve feet high
I saw a cottage near the sky
I saw a balloon made of lead
I saw a coffin drop down dead
I saw two sparrows run a race
I saw two horses making lace
I saw a girl just like a cat
I saw a kitten wear a hat
I saw a man who saw these, too,
And said though strange they were all true.

THE RABBIT

The rabbit has a charming face:
Its private life is a disgrace.
I really dare not name to you
The awful things that rabbits do;
Things that your paper never prints –
You only mention them in hints.
They have such lost, degraded souls
No wonder they inhabit holes;
When such depravity is found
It only can live underground.

THE ELEPHANT

The Elephant is a bonny bird,
It flies from bough to bough,
It makes its nest in a rhubarb tree,
And whistles like a cow.

ADVERTISEMENT

The codfish lays a million eggs,
The helpful hen lays one,
The codfish makes no fuss of its achievement,
The hen boasts what she's done.
We forget the gentle codfish,
The hen we eulogise,
Which teaches us this lesson: that
It pays to advertise.

AND SO FAREWELL

SHE IS GONE

You can shed tears that she is gone
or you can smile because she has lived.

You can close your eyes and pray that she'll come back
or you can open your eyes and see all she's left.

Your heart can be empty because you can't see her
or you can be full of the love you shared.

You can turn your back on tomorrow and live yesterday
or you can be happy for tomorrow because of yesterday.

You can remember her and only that she's gone
or you can cherish her memory and let it live on.

You can cry and close your mind, be empty and turn
     your back
or you can do what she'd want: smile, open your eyes,
     love and go on.

THE PARTING GLASS

Oh all the time that e'er I spent,
I spent it in good company;
And any harm that e'er I've done,
I trust it was to none but me;
May those I've loved through all the years
Have memories now they'll e'er recall;
So fill to me the parting glass,
Goodnight, and joy be with you all.

Oh all the comrades that e'er I had,
Are sorry for my going away;
And all the loved ones that e'er I had
Would wish me one more day to stay.
But since it falls unto my lot
That I should leave and you should not,
I'll gently rise and I'll softly call
Goodnight, and joy be with you all.

Of all good times that e'er we shared,
I leave to you fond memory;
And for all the friendship that e'er we had
I ask you to remember me;

And when you sit and stories tell,
I'll be with you and help recall;
So fill to me the parting glass,
God bless, and joy be with you all.

ALWAYS WITH YOU

Your mother is always with you.
She's the whisper of the leaves
as you walk down the street.
She's the smell of bleach
in your freshly laundered socks.
She's the cool hand on your brow
When you're not well.
Your mother lives inside your laughter.
She's crystallized in every teardrop.
She's the place you came from,
your first home.
She's the map you follow
with every step that you take.
She's your first love
and your first heartbreak ...
and nothing on earth can separate you.

THE DAY YOU LEFT

With tears we saw you suffer,
As we watched you fade away,
Our hearts were almost broken,
As you fought so hard to stay.
We knew you had to leave us,
But you did not go alone,
For part of us went with you
The day you left your home.

GOD'S GARDEN

God looked around his garden
and found an empty space.
Then he looked down upon the earth
and saw your tired face.
He put his arms around you
and lifted you to rest.
God's garden must be beautiful
for He only takes the best.
He knew that you were suffering.
He knew you were in pain.
He knew you never would get well
upon this earth again.
He saw the roads were getting rough
and the hills were hard to climb,
So he closed your weary eyes
and whispered 'Peace be thine'.
It broke my heart to lose you
But you did not go alone
For part of me went with you
the day God called you home.

A CHILD LOANED

'I'll lend you for a little time a child of Mine,' he said,
'For you to love the while she lives, and mourn for
    when she's dead.
She may be six or seven weeks, or thirteen years,
    or three,
But will you, till I call her back, take care of her
    for Me?
She'll bring her charm to gladden you, and should
    her stay be brief,
You'll have her lovely memories as solace for
    your grief.
I cannot promise she will stay, since all from
    Earth return,
But there are lessons taught down there I want this
    child to learn.
I looked the wide world over in my search for
    teachers true,
And from the throngs who crowd life's lanes I have
    selected you.
Now will you give her all your love, nor think the
    labour's vain,
Nor hate me when I come to call and take her
    back again?'
I fancied that I heard them say, 'Dear Lord, Thy will
    be done,
For all the joys Thy child shall bring the risk of grief
    we'll run.
We'll shelter her with tenderness, we'll love her
    while we may
And for the happiness we've known, forever
    grateful stay.

But, should the angels call for her much sooner than
    we planned
We'll brave the bitter grief that comes and try
    to understand.'

NOT HOW DID HE DIE

Not how did he die, but how did he live?
Not what did he gain, but what did he give?
These are the units to measure the worth
Of a man as a man, regardless of birth.
Not what was his church or what was his creed,
But had he befriended those really in need?
Not what was his station, but had he a heart?
How did he play his God-given part?
Was he ever ready, with word of good cheer,
To bring back a smile, to banish a tear?
Not how did the formal obituary run?
But how many grieved when his life's work was done?

WILLY DROWNED IN YARROW

Down in yon garden sweet and gay
    Where bonnie grows the lily,
I heard a fair maid sighing say,
    'My wish be wi' sweet Willie!

'Willie's rare, and Willie's fair,
    And Willie's wondrous bonny;
And Willie hecht to marry me
    Gin e'er he married ony.

'O gentle wind, that bloweth south,
    From where my Love repaireth,
Convey a kiss frae his dear mouth
    And tell me how he fareth!

'O tell sweet Willie to come doun
    And hear the mavis singing,
And see the birds on ilka bush
    And leaves around them hinging.

'The lav'rock there, wi' her white breast
    And gentle throat sae narrow;
There's sport eneuch for gentlemen
    On leader haughs and Yarrow.

'O Leader haughs are wide and braid
    And Yarrow haughs are bonny;
There Willie hecht to marry me
    If e'er he married ony.

'But Willie's gone, whom I thought on,
    And does not hear me weeping;
Draws many a tear frae true love's e'e
    When other maids are sleeping.

'Yestreen I made my bed fu' braid,
    The night I'll mak' it narrow,
For a' the live-lang winter night
    I lie twined o' my marrow.

'O came ye by yon water-side?
    Pou'd you the rose or lily?
Or came you by yon meadow green
    Or saw you my sweet Willie?'

She sought him up, she sought him down,
    She sought him braid and narrow;
Syne, in the cleaving of a craig,
    She found him drown'd in Yarrow!

GOD CALLED YOUR NAME SO SOFTLY

God called your name so softly
That only you could hear
And no one heard the footsteps
Of angels drawing near
It broke our hearts to lose you
But you did not go alone
For part of us went with you
The day God called you home.

INDIAN PRAYER

When I am dead
Cry for me a little,
Think of me sometimes,
But not too much.
Think of me now and again
As I was in life
At some moments it's pleasant to recall,
But not for long.
Leave me in peace
And I shall leave you in peace,
And while you live
Let your thoughts be with the living.

THE END OF THE ROAD

When I come to the end of the road
And the sun has set for me
I want no tears in a gloom-filled room –
Why cry for a soul set free?

Miss me a little, but not too much
And not with your head bowed low
Remember the love that once we shared
Miss me, but let me go.

For this is a journey we all must make
And each must go alone
It's all part of God's perfect plan
A step on the road to home.

When you are lonely and sick of heart
Go to the friends that we know
And bury your sorrows in doing good.
Miss me, but let me go.

I ONLY WANTED YOU

They say memories are golden,
Well maybe that is true,
I never wanted memories,
I only wanted you.
A million times I needed you,
A million times I cried,
If love alone could have saved you
You never would have died.
In life I loved you dearly,
In death I love you still.
In my heart you hold a place
No one could ever fill.
If tears could build a stairway
And heartache make a lane,
I'd walk the path to heaven
And bring you back again.
Our family chain is broken,
And nothing seems the same.
But as God calls us one by one,
The chain will link again.

GOD MAKE ME BRAVE

God make me brave –
Let me strengthen after pain
As a tree strengthens after rain
Shining and lovely again.
As a blown grass lifts, let me rise
From sorrow with quiet eyes
Knowing Thy way is wise
God make me braver – life brings
Such blinding things!
Help me keep Thee in my sight,
That out of dark – comes light.

THE DASH BETWEEN THE YEARS

I read of a man who stood to speak
At the funeral of his friend.
He referred to the dates on his tombstone
From the beginning to the end.
He noted that first came his date of birth
And he spoke the following date with tears.
But he said what mattered most of all
Was the dash between those years.
For that dash represents all the time
That he spent alive on earth
And now only those who loved him
Know what the little line is worth.
For it matters not how much we own,
The cars, the house, the cash,
What matters is how we live and love
And how we spent our dash.

So think about this long and hard
Are there things you'd like to change?
For you never know how much time is left
That can still be rearranged.
If we could just slow down enough
To consider what's true and real
And always try to understand
The way other people feel,
And be less quick to anger,
And show appreciation more,
And love the people in our lives
Like we've never loved before.
If we treat each other with respect
And more often wear a smile
Remembering that this special dash
Might only last a little while.
So, when your eulogy is being read
With your life's actions to rehash
Would you be proud of the things they say
About how you spent your dash?

DO NOT BE AFRAID

Do not stand at my grave and weep
I am not there, I do not sleep.
I am a thousand winds that blow,
I am the diamond glint on snow.
I am the sunlight on ripened grain,
I am the gentle autumn rain.
When you wake in the morning hush
I am the swift, uplifting rush
of quiet birds in circling flight.
I am the soft starlight at night.
Do not stand at my grave and weep
I am not there – I do not sleep.

THE COMMEMORATION

In the rising of the sun and in its going down,
    We remember them.
In the blowing of the wind and in the chill of winter,
    We remember them.
In the blueness of the sky and in the warmth of summer,
    We remember them.
In the rustling of leaves and in the beauty of autumn,
    We remember them.
In the beginning of the year and when it ends,
    We remember them.
When we are lost and sick at heart,
    We remember them.
When we have joys we long to share,
    We remember them.
So long as we live, they, too, shall live, for they are
    part of us,
And we remember them.

ALL'S WELL THAT ENDS WELL

A Friend of mine was married to a scold,
To me he came, and all his troubles told.
Said he, 'She's like a woman raving mad.'
'Alas! My friend,' said I, 'that's very bad!'
'No, not so bad,' said he; 'for, with her, true
I had both house and land, and money too.'
    'That was well,' said I;
    'No, not so well,' said he;
    'For I and her own brother
    Went to law with one another;
    I was cast, the suit was lost,
And every penny went to pay the cost.'
    'That was bad,' said I;
    'No, not so bad,' said he:
'For we agreed that he the house should keep,
And give to me four score of Yorkshire sheep
All fat, and fair, and fine, they were to be.'
'Well, then,' said I, 'sure that was well for thee?'
    'No, not so well,' said he;
    'For, when the sheep I got,
    They every one died of the rot.
    'That was bad,' said I;
    'No, not so bad,' said he;
    'For I had thought to scrape the fat
    And keep it in an oaken vat;
Then into tallow melt for winter store,'
'Well, then,' said I, 'that's better than before?'
    ''Twas not so well,' said he;
    'For having got a clumsy fellow
    To scrape the fat and melt the tallow;

Into the melting fat the fire catches,
    And, like brimstone matches,
Burnt my house to ashes.'
    'That was bad,' said I;
'No! no so bad,' said he; 'for, what is best,
My scolding wife has gone among the rest.'

AND SO FAREWELL

Thy journey be auspicious; may the breeze,
Gentle and soothing, fan thy cheek;
May lakes all bright with lily cups delight thine eye,
The sunbeam's heat be cooled by shady trees,
The dust beneath thy feet the pollen be
Of lotuses.

WAR

SONG OF THE ENGLISH BOWMEN

Agincourt, Agincourt!
Know ye not Agincourt,
Where English slew and hurt
All their French foemen?
With their pikes and bills brown,
How the French were beat down,
Shot by our Bowmen!

Agincourt, Agincourt!
Know ye not Agincourt,
Never to be forgot,
Or known to no men?
Where English cloth-yard Arrows,
Killed the French like tame sparrows,
Slain by our Bowmen!

Agincourt, Agincourt!
Know ye not Agincourt,
English of every sort,
High men and low men,
Fought that day wondrous well,
All our old stories tell,
Thanks to our Bowmen!

Agincourt, Agincourt!
Know ye not Agincourt?
Where our fifth Harry taught
Frenchmen to know men:
And when the day was done,
Thousands fell to one
Good English Bowman!

Agincourt, Agincourt!
Know ye not Agincourt?
Dear was the victory bought
    By fifty yeomen
Ask any English wench,
They were worth all the French:
Rare English Bowmen!

A CAROL OF AGINCOURT

Deo gracias, Anglia,
Redde pro victoria.

Oure kinge went forth to Normandy
With grace and might of chivalry.
Ther God for him wrought mervelusly:
Wherefore Engloride may calle and cry.

He sette a sege, the soothe for to say,
To Harflu towne with ryal array:
That towne he wan and made affray
That Fraunce shall riwe till Domesday.

Than went oure kinge with alle his hoste
Thorwe Fraunce, for alle the Frenshe boste:
He spared, no drede, of lest ne moste,
Till he come to Agincourt coste.

Than, forsoth, that knight comely
In Agincourt feld he faught manly.
Thorw grace of God most mighty
He had bothe the felde and the victory.

There dukis and erlis, lorde and barone,
Where take and slaine, and that well sone,
And summe were ladde into Lundone
With joye and merthe and grete renone.

Now gracious God he save oure kinge,
His peple and alle his well-willinge:
Yef him gode life and gode ending,
That we with merthe mowe safely singe.

THE BRITISH GRENADIERS

Some talk of Alexander, and some of Hercules.
Of Hector and Lysander, and such great names
    as these;
But of all the world's brave heroes, there's none that
    can compare,
With a tow, row row, row row, row row, to the
    British Grenadier.

Those heroes of antiquity ne'er saw a cannon ball,
Or knew the force of powder to slay their foes withal;
But our brave boys do know it, and banish all
    their fears,
Sing tow, row row, row row, row row, to the
    British Grenadiers.

Then Jove, the god of thunder, and Mars, the god
    of war,
Brave Neptune with his trident, Apollo in his car,
And all the gods celestial, descending from
    their sphere,
Behold with admiration the British Grenadier.

Whene'er we are commanded to storm the palisades;
Our leaders march with fusees, and we with
    hand-grenades,
We throw them from the glacis, about the
    Frenchmen's ears,
With a tow, row row, row row, row row, for the
    British Grenadiers.

And when the siege is over, we to the town repair,
The townsmen cry huzza, boys, here comes a grenadier,
Here come the grenadiers, my boys, who know no
    doubts or fears,
Then sing tow, row row, row row, row row, for the
    British Grenadiers.

SWEET POLLY OLIVER

As sweet Polly Oliver lay musing in bed,
A sudden strange fancy came into her head:
'Nor mother nor father shall make me false prove,
I'll 'list for a soldier and follow my love.

So early next morning she softly arose
And dressed herself up in the dead brother's clothes.
She cut her hair close and she stained her face brown,
And went for a soldier to fair London town.

Then up spoke the sergeant one day at his drill:
'Now who's good for nursing? A captain, he's ill.'
'I'm ready,' said Polly. To nurse him she's gone,
And finds it's her true love, all wasted and wan.

The first week the doctor kept shaking his head.
'No nursing, young fellow, can save him,' he said;
But when Polly Oliver had nursed him back to life,
He cried, 'You have cherished him as if you were
    his wife.'

O then Polly Oliver, she burst into tears
And told the good doctor her hopes and her fears,
And very shortly after, for better or for worse,
The captain took joyfully his pretty soldier nurse.

MY SODGER LADDIE

My yellow mou'd mistress, I bid you adieu,
For I've been too long in slavery with you,
With washing and scouring I'm seldom in bedy
And now I will go with my sodger laddie,
My sodger laddie, my sodger laddie,
The kisses are sweet of a sodger laddie.

With the crust of your loaf, and dregs of your tea,
You fed you lap doggie far better than me,
With rinning and spinning, my head was unsteady,
But now I will go with my sodger laddie.

For yarn, for yarn, you always did cry,
And look'd to my pirn, ay as ye went by;
Now the drums they do beat, and my bundle is ready,
And I'll go along with my sodger laddie.

I'll always be ready, with needle and soap,
For possing and patching to serve the whole troop,
I'll be loving and kind, and live like a lady,
When I go abroad with my sodger laddie.

In heat of battles, I'll keep on the flank,
With a stone in a stocking, and give them a clank,
If he be knocked down, though he be my daddy,
I'll bring all his clink to my sodger laddie.

For robbing the dead is no thievish trick,
I'll rifle his breeches, and then his knapsack,
But yet on a friend I'll not be so ready,
If he's been acquaint with my sodger laddie.

FAR AWAY

Around her leg she wore a purple garter,
> She wore it in the springtime and in the month
> of May.
And if you asked her why the hell she wore it,
> She wore it for an airman who is far, far away.

Around the block she pushed a baby carriage,
> She pushed it in the springtime and in the month
> of May,
And if you asked her why the hell she pushed it,
> She pushed it for an airman who is far, far away.

Behind the door her father kept a shotgun,
> He kept it in the springtime and in the month
> of May,
And if you asked him why the hell he kept it,
> He kept it for an airman who is far, far away.

Upon his grave she placed a bunch of flowers,
> She placed it in the springtime and in the month
> of May,
And if you asked her why the hell she placed it,
> She placed it for an airman who is six feet down.

ARTHUR McBRIDE

I once knew a fellow named Arthur McBride,
And he and I rambled down by the seaside,
A-looking for pleasure or what might betide,
And the weather was pleasant and charming.

So gaily and gallant we went on our tramp,
And we met Sergeant Harper and Corporal Cramp,
And the little wee fellow who roused up the camp
With his row-de-dow-dow in the morning.

Good morning, young fellows, the sergeant he cried.
And the same to you, sergeant, was all our reply.
There was nothing more spoken, we made to pass by,
And continue our walk in the morning.

Well now, my fine fellows, if you will enlist,
A guinea in gold I will slap in your fist,
And a crown in the bargain to kick up the dust
And drink the Queen's health in the morning.

Oh no, mister sergeant, we aren't for sale,
We'll make no such bargain, and your bribe won't avail.
We're not tired of our country, and don't care to sail,
Though your offer is pleasant and charming.

If we were such fools as to take your advance,
It's right bloody slender would be our poor chance,
For the Queen wouldn't scruple to send us to France
And get us all shot in the morning.

Ha, now, you young blackguards, if you say one
    more word,
I swear by the herrins, I'll draw out my sword
And run through your bodies as my strength may afford.
So now, you young buggers, take warning.

Well, we beat that bold drummer as flat as a shoe,
And we make a football of his row-de-dow-do,
And as for the others we knocked out the two.
Oh, we were the boys in that morning.

We took the old weapons that hung by their side
And flung them as far as we could in the tide.
May the devil go with you, says Arthur McBride,
For delaying our walk this fine morning.

AN OLD SOLDIER OF THE QUEEN'S

Of an old Soldier of the Queen's,
With an old motley coat, and a Malmsey nose,
And an old jerkin that's out at the elbows,
And an old pair of boots, drawn on without hose
Stuft with rags instead of toes;
    And an old Soldier of the Queen's
    And the Queen's old Soldier.

With an old rusty sword that's hackt with blows,
And an old dagger to scare away the crows,
And an old horse that reels as he goes,
And an old saddle that no man knows,
    And an old Soldier of the Queen's
    And the Queen's old Soldier.

With his old wounds in Eighty Eight,
Which he recover'd, at Tilbury fight;
With an old Passport that never was read,
That in his old travels stood him in great stead;
    And an old Soldier of the Queen's,
    And the Queen's old Soldier.

With his old gun, and his bandeliers,
And an old head-piece to keep warm his ears,
With an old shirt is grown to wrack,
With a huge louse, with a great list on his back,
Is able to carry a pedlar and his pack;
    And an old Soldier of the Queen's,
    And the Queen's old Soldier.

REGATTA

The Little Ships of England,
In fifteen eighty-eight,
The Armada in the Channel,
King Philip at the gate.
From Sussex and from Hampshire
Sailed out with pennons high,
Like terriers at the heels of Drake,
The furious fighting ships of Drake,
To victual and supply.

Three hundred years and over,
Drew onward to a day,
The foe across the Channel,
Our fighting men at bay.
Ghostly, through listening shires
Drake's drum began to roll,
Like terriers at the Navy's heels,
The Little Ships on dauntless keels,
Set out with steadfast soul.

The Little Ships of Dunkirk,
Drove forward into hell,
Death on the beaches, death from the air,
Machine-gun, bomb and shell.
Yachts, trawler, barge and coaster,
Battered and scored and black,
Snatched life like Lazarus from the tomb,
Snatched victory from the jaws of doom,
And brought the Army back.

A SOLDIER STOOD AT THE PEARLY GATE

A soldier stood at the pearly gate
His face was scarred and old.
He stood before the man of fate
For admission to the fold.

'What have you done,' St Peter asked,
'To gain admission here?'
'I've been a soldier, sir,' he said
'For many and many a year.'

The pearly gate swung open wide
As Peter touched the bell
'Inside,' he said, 'and choose your harp
You've had your share of hell.'

MILITARY ABC

A stands for ATTENTION, the first word he knows,
And B stands for BULLET, to tickle his foes.
C stands for a CHARGE, which the Frenchmen
    all dread;
And D stands for DISCHARGE, which soon lays
    them dead.
Next E begins EASE, at which sometimes he stands;
And F bids to FIGHT, when our enemy lands.
G stands for GENERAL, GRAPESHOT and GUN,
Which together combined must make Bonaparte run.
Then H brings HONOUR, to soldiers full dear;
And J stands for JUSTICE, which next they revere.
But K bids them KILL, for their country and King,
For whose health each true Briton doth joyfully sing.
L is LOVE, which the soldier will often times feel,
And M bids him MERCY, when conqu'ror, to deal.
N stands for a NATION, of Englishmen free;
And O for OUTPOST – but ours is the sea.
The P stands for PICKET, and for POINEEER;
And Q shows our enemies QUAKING with fear.
Next R stands for REGIMENT and ROLL of the drums;
And S for SALUTE when the general comes
So T both for TOUCH-HOLE and TRIGGER may stand;
And V for the brave VOLUNTEERS of this land.
Then W whispers that WAR soon may cease:
And X, Y and Z will rejoice at the peace.

WHY ARE THEY SELLING POPPIES?

'Why are they selling poppies, Mummy,
Selling poppies in town today?'
'The poppies, child, are flowers of love
For the men who marched away.'
'But why have they chosen a poppy, Mummy,
Why not a beautiful rose?'
'Because, my child, men fought and died
In the fields where the poppy grows.'
'But why are the poppies red, Mummy,
Why are the poppies so red?'
'Red is the colour of blood, my child,
The blood our soldiers shed.'
'The heart of the poppy is black, Mummy,
Why does it have to be black?'
'Black, my child, is the symbol of grief
For the men who never came back.'
'But why, Mummy, are you crying so?
Your tears are giving you pain.'
'My tears are my fears for you, my child,
For the world is – FORGETTING AGAIN.'

ON MARY ANN

Mary Ann has gone to rest,
Safe at last on Abraham's breast,
Which may be nuts for Mary Ann,
But is certainly rough on Abraham.

OVER THE HILLS AND FAR AWAY

Hark, now the drums beat up again,
For all true soldier gentlemen,
Then let us 'list and march, I say,
Over the hills and far away.
Over the hills and o'er the main,
To Flanders, Portugal and Spain,
Queen Anne commands and we'll obey,
Over the hills and far away.

AN AA GUNNER LAY DYING

An AA gunner lay dying
At the end of a midsummer's day.
His comrades were gathered around him
To carry his fragments away.

The mounting was piled on his wishbone,
The breech-block was wrapped round his head,
A shell stuck out of his elbow,
It was plain that he'd shortly be dead.

He spat out a toggle and rammer
And stirred in the oil where he lay.
Then to his poor mournful comrades
These brave parting words did he say:

'Take the rollers out of my stomach,
'Take the breech-block out of my neck,
'Remove from my kidneys the handwheel.
'There's lots of good parts in this wreck.'
'Take the chase out of my gullet,
'Take the interceptor out of my brain,
'Extract from my liver the striker,
'And assemble the pom-pom again.'

'I'll be riding a cloud in the morning,
'And aircraft no more shall I fear,
'And high on a cloud over Scapa
'I'll shed all my good friends a tear.'

'So don't mourn too much over my body.
'Damn old Hitler and all of his lies.
'Here's a health to the dead already.
'Let's hope he's the next one who dies.'

A SOLDIER – HIS PRAYER

Stay with me God. The night is dark,
The night is cold: my little spark
Of courage dies. The night is long;
Be with me God, and make me strong.

I love a game. I love a fight.
I hate the dark; I love the light,
I love my child; I love my wife,
I am no coward, I love Life.

Life with its change of mood and shade,
I want to live. I'm not afraid,
But me and mine are hard to part;
Oh, unknown God, lift up my heart.

You stilled the waters at Dunkirk
And saved Your Servants. All your work
Is wonderful, Dear God. You strode
Before us down that dreadful road.

We were alone, and hope had fled;
We loved our country and our dead,
And could not shame them; so we stayed
The Course, and were not much afraid.

Dear God, that nightmare road! And then
That Sea! We got there … we were men
My eyes were blind, my feet were torn,
My soul sang like a bird at dawn!

I knew that death is but a door.
I knew what we were fighting for:
Peace for the kids our brothers freed,
A kinder world, a cleaner breed.

I'm but the son my mother bore,
A simple man, and nothing more,
But – God of strength and gentleness,
Be pleased to make me nothing less.

Help me, O God, when Death is near
To mock the haggard face of fear,
That when I fall – if fall I must –
My soul may triumph in the Dust.

EVERY BULLET HAS ITS BILLET

I'm a tough true-hearted sailor,
    Careless and all that, d'ye see,
Never at the times a railer –
    What is time or tide to me?
All must die when fate shall will it,
    Providence ordains it so;
Every bullet has its billet,
    Man the boat, boys – Yeo, heave yeo,

Life's at best a sea of trouble,
    He who fears it is a dunce;
Death to me's an empty bubble,
    I can never die but once.
Blood, if duty bids, I'll spill it:
    Yet I have a tear for woe;
Every bullet has its billet,
    Man the boat, boys – Yeo, heave yeo.

Shrouded in a hammock, glory
    Celebrates the falling brave;
Oh! how many, famed in story,
    Sleep below in ocean's cave.
Bring the can, boys – let us fill it;
    Shall we shun the fight? O, no!
Every bullet has its billet,
    Man the boat, boys – Yeo, heave yeo.

CHRISTMAS

GUESTS

Yet if His majesty, our sovereign lord,
Should of his own accord
Friendly himself invite,
And say, 'I'll be your guest to-morrow night,'
How should we stir ourselves, call and command
All hands to work! 'Let no man idle stand!

'Set me fine Spanish tables in the hall;
See they be fitted all;
Let there be room to eat
And order taken that there want no meat.
See every sconce and candlestick made bright,
That without tapers they may give a light.

'Look to the presence: are the carpets spread,
The dazie o'er the head,
The cushions in the chairs,
And all the candles lighted on the stairs?
Perfume the chambers, and in any case
Let each man give attendance in his place!'

Thus, if a king were coming, would we do;
And 'twere good reason too;

For 'tis a duteous thing
To show all honour to an earthly king,
And after all our travail and our cost,
So he be pleased, to think no labour lost.

But at the coming of the King of Heaven
All's set at six and seven;
We wallow in our sin,
Christ cannot find a chamber in the inn.
We entertain Him always like a stranger,
And, as at first, still lodge Him in the manger.

SANTA CLAUS

He comes in the night! He comes in the night!
    He softly, silently comes;
While the little brown heads on the pillows so white
    Are dreaming of bugles and drums.
He cuts through the snow like a ship through the foam,
    While the white flakes around him whirl;
Who tells him I know not, but he findeth the home
    Of each good little boy and girl.

His sleigh it is long, and deep, and wide;
    It will carry a host of things,
While dozens of drums hang over the side,
        With the sticks sticking under the strings.
And yet not the sound of a drum is heard,
    Not a bugle blast is blown,
As he mounts to the chimney-top like a bird,
    And drops to the hearth like a stone.

The little red stockings he silently fills,
  Till the stockings will hold no more;
The bright little sleds for the great snow hills
  Are quickly set down on the floor.
Then Santa Claus mounts to the roof like a bird,
  And glides to his seat in the sleigh;
Not the sound of a bugle or drum is heard
  As he noiselessly gallops away.

He rides to the East, and he rides to the West,
  Of his goodies he touches not one;
He eateth the crumbs of the Christmas feast
  When the dear little folks are done.
Old Santa Claus doeth all that he can;
  This beautiful mission is his;
Then, children, be good to the little old man,
  When you find who the little man is.

CAROL FROM THE CHESTER MYSTERY PLAY

He who made the earth so fair
Slumbers in a stable bare
Warmed by cattle standing there.

Oxen, lowing, stand all round,
To the stall no other sound
Mars the peace by Mary found.

Joseph piles the soft, sweet hay,
Starlight drives the dark away,
Angels sing a heavenly lay.

Jesus sleeps in Mary's arms,
Sheltered there from rude alarm,
None can do Him ill or harm.

See His mother o'er Him bend,
Hers the joy to soothe and tend,
Here the bliss that knows no end.

SANTA'S PREPARATION

'Are the reindeer in the rain, dear?'
Asked Mrs Santa Claus.
'No, I put them in the barn, dear,
To dry their little paws.'
'Is the sleigh, sir, put away, sir
In the barn beside the deer?'
'Yes, I'm going to get it ready
To use again next year.'

'And the pack, dear, is it back dear?'
'Yes it's empty of its toys,
And tomorrow I'll start filling it
For next year's girls and boys.'

THIS HAPPY CHRISTMAS DAY

Roast the turkey,
    Decorate the tree;
Jesus born in Bethlehem,
    Joy for you and me.

Trudge the winter's snow,
    Merry carols sing;
Jesus born in Bethlehem,
    God's little Saviour King.
Bitterness and strife,
    This world must cast away;
Jesus born in Bethlehem
    This happy Christmas Day.

JESUS, OUR BROTHER (THE FRIENDLY BEASTS)

Jesus, our Brother, strong and good
Was humbly born in a stable rude,
And the friendly beasts around Him stood.
Jesus, our Brother, strong and good.

'I,' said the donkey, shaggy and brown,
'I carried His Mother up hill and down.
I carried Her safely to Bethlehem town.
I,' said the donkey, shaggy and brown.

'I,' said the cow, all white and red,
'I gave Him my manger for his bed.
I gave Him my hay to pillow His head.
I,' said the cow, all white and red.

'I,' said the sheep with curly horn,
'I gave Him my wool for His blanket warm.
He wore my coat on Christmas morn.
I,' said the sheep with curly horn.

'I' said the dove from the rafters high,
'Cooed Him to sleep, my mate and I.
We cooed Him to sleep, my mate and I.
I,' said the dove from the rafters high.

And every beast, by some good spell,
In the stable dark was glad to tell
Of the gift he gave Emmanuel,
The gift he gave Emmanuel.

THE SHEPHERD

I have sat beside my flock and watched
Time march across a velvet sky;
Have witnessed seasons ebb and flow:
Have seen life born, grow old and die.
And once, 'twas long ago, I saw
Above me in the vault of night,
A nascent star, all pure sublime,
That pierced the firmament with light.
Other shepherds, just a few miles hence,
Have sworn they heard the heavens ring
With angel voices, heralds, jubilant,
Who brought them tiding of a new-born King.
They heard the news and straightaway travelled fast
To Bethlehem where, it is said,
They found the babe in swaddling clothes
Within a lowly cattle shed.
I did not see what those men saw,
Their feelings, too, I did not share;
But often, when I sit alone
I wish to God that I'd been there.

WASSAILING SONG

Wisselton, wasselton, who lives here?
We've come to taste your Christmas beer.
Up the kitchen and down the hall,
Holly, ivy, and mistletoe;
A peck of apples will serve us all,
Give us some apples and let us go.

Up with your stocking, on with your shoe,
If you haven't any apples, money will do.
My carol's done, and I must be gone,
No longer can I stay here.
God bless you all, great and small,
And send you a happy new year.

CHRISTMAS CAROL

God bless the master of this house,
    Likewise the mistress, too:
And all the little children
    That round the table go.
Love and joy come to you,
    And to you your wassail, too,
And God bless you and send you
    A happy New Year.

AS JOSEPH WAS A-WALKING

As Joseph was a-walking
    He heard an angel sing:
'This night shall be born
    Our heavenly king.

'He neither shall be born
    In housen nor in hall,
Nor in the place of Paradise,
    But in an ox's stall.

'He neither shall be clothed
    In purple nor in pall,
But all in fair linen,
    As were babies all.

'He neither shall be rocked
    In silver nor in gold,
But in a wooden cradle
    That rocks on the mould.

'He neither shall be christened
    In white wine or red,
But with fair spring water,
    With which we were christened.'

I SING THE BIRTH WAS BORN TONIGHT

I sing the birth was born tonight,
    The author both of Life and Light.
    The angels so did sound it.
And like the revised shepherds said
    Who saw the light and were afraid
    Yet searched, and true they found it.

The Son of God, the Eternal King
    That did us all salvation bring
    And freed the soul from danger.
He whom the whole world could not take
    The Word, which Heaven and Earth did make
    Was now laid in a manger.

The Father's wisdom willed it so;
    The Son's obedience knew no 'No!'
    Both wills were in one stature.
And as that wisdom had decreed
    The Word was now made flesh indeed
    And took on Him our nature.

What comfort by Him do we win
    Who made himself the price of sin
    To make us heirs of glory.
To see this babe all innocence
    A martyr born in our defence.
    Can man forget this story?

THE STORKE CAROL

The storke she rose on Christmas Eve
And sayde unto her broode,
I now must far to Bethlehem
To view the sonne of God.
She gave to each his dole of mete,
She stowed them farely in,
And far she flew and fast she flew
And came to Bethlehem.

Nowe where is He of David's line
She asked at house and halle?
He is not here, they spoke hardly,
But in a mangier stalle.
She found Him in a mangier stalle
With that most Holy Mayde,
The gentle storke, she wept to see
The Lord so rudely layde.

Then from her panting breast she plucked
The feathers white and warm,
She strewed them in the manger bed
To keep the Lord from harm.
'Nowe blessed be the gentle storke
For evermore,' quote He,
'For that she saw my sad estate
And showed such pity.'

'Full welcome shall she ever be
In hamlet and in halle,
And called henceforth the blessed bird
And friend of babies alle.

AT THE SIGN OF THE HEART

But art Thou come, dear Saviour? Hath Thy love
Thus made Thee stoop, and leave Thy throne above

Thy lofty heavens, and thus thyself to dress
In dust to visit mortals? Could no less
A condescension serve? And after all
The mean reception of a cratch and stall?

Dear Lord, I'll fetch Thee thence! I have a room
('Tis poor, but 'tis my best) if Thou wilt come

Within so small a cell, where I would fain
Mine and the world's Redeemer entertain,
I mean, my Heart: 'tis sluttish, I confess,
And will not mend Thy lodging, Lord, unless

Thou send before Thy harbinger, I mean
Thy pure and purging Grace, to make it clean

And sweep its nasty corners; then I'll try
To wash it also with a weeping eye.

And when 'tis swept and wash'd, I then will go
And, with Thy leave, I'll fetch some flowers that grow
In Thine own garden, Faith and Love, to Thee;
With these I'll dress it up, and these shall be
My rosemary and bays. Yet when my best
Is done, the room's not fit for such a Guest.

But here's the cure; Thy presence, Lord, alone
Will make a stall a Court, a cratch a Throne.

157

THE NATURAL WORLD

ENGLISH COUNTRY GARDENS

How many kinds of sweet flowers grow
In an English country garden?
We'll tell you now of some that we know,
Those we miss you'll surely pardon.
Daffodils, heart's-ease and flox,
Meadowsweet and lady smocks,
Gentian, lupine and tall hollyhocks,
Roses, foxgloves, snowdrops, blue forget-me-nots
In an English country garden.

How many insects come here and go
In an English country garden?
We'll tell you now of some that we know,
Those we miss you'll surely pardon.
Fireflies, moths, gnats and bees,
Spiders climbing in the trees,
Butterflies drift in the gentle breeze,
There are snakes, ants that sting
And other creeping things
In an English country garden.

How many songbirds fly to and fro
In an English country garden?
We'll tell you now of some that we know,

Those we miss you'll surely pardon.
Bobolink, cuckoo and quail,
Tanager and cardinal,
Bluebird, lark, thrush and nightingale.
There is joy in the spring
When the birds begin to sing
In an English country garden.

BLUEBELLS

In the bluebell forest
There is scarce a sound,
Only bluebells growing
Everywhere around.

I can't see a blackbird
Or a thrush to sing,
I think I can almost
Hear the bluebells ring.

DOUBLE TIME

March is a jade, a fickle thing,
With the winter's wind and the sun of spring.
The sun writes, 'Come!' and the wind says, 'Go!'
The sun writes, 'Rain!' and the wind says, 'Snow!'
The sun keeps writing, the wind erasing,
And March never knows which way she's facing.

BUDS

The chestnut buds are
    very brown,
And very sticky, too;
They always turn towards
    the sun
That shines amid the blue.

The little buds that dress
    in black,
There's no mistaking these;
They grow upon the old
    ash tree
That's waving in the breeze.

And what about these pointed buds,
Which everyone must know?
They're children of the big
    beach tree,
Whose leaves have such a glow.

BIRD'S NESTS

The skylark's nest among the grass
And waving corn is found;
The robin's on a shady bank,
With oak leaves strewn around.

The wren builds in an ivied thorn
Or old and ruined wall;
The mossy nest so covered in,
You scarce can see at all.

The martins build their nests of clay,
In rows beneath the eaves;
While silvery lichens, moss and hair,
The chaffinch interweaves.

The cuckoo makes no nest at all,
But through the wood she strays
Until she finds one snug and warm,
And there her egg she lays.

The sparrow has a nest of hay,
With feathers warmly lined;
The ring-dove's careless nest of sticks
On lofty trees we find.

Rooks build together in a wood,
And often disagree;
The owl will build inside a barn
Or in a hollow tree.

The blackbird's nest of grass and mud
In brush and bank is found;
The lapwing's darkly spotted eggs
Are laid upon the ground.

The magpie's nest is girt with thorns
In leafless tree or hedge;
The wild duck and the water-hen
Build by the water's edge.

Birds build their nests from year to year,
According to their kind,
Some very neat and beautiful
Some easily designed.

LITTLE BY LITTLE

'Little by Little,' an acorn said,
As it slowly sank in its mossy bed,
'I am improving every day,
Hidden deep in the earth away.'

Little by little each day it grew,
Little by little it sipped the dew;
Downward it sent a thread-like root,
Up in the air sprang a tiny shoot.

Day after day, and year after year,
Little by little the leaves appear;
And the slender branches spread far and wide,
Till the mighty oak is the forest's pride.

'Little by little,' said a thoughtful boy,
'Each precious moment I will employ,
And always this rule in my mind shall dwell:
Whatever I do, I'll do it well.

'Little by little, I'll learn to know
The treasured wisdom of long ago;
And sometime, perhaps, the world will be
Happier and better because of me.'

THE BLACKBIRD

In midst of woods or pleasant grove
    Where all sweet birds do sing,
Methought I heard so rare a sound,
    Which made the heavens to ring.
The charm was good, the noise full sweet,
    Each bird did play his part;
And I admired to hear the same;
Joy sprung into my heart.

The blackbird made the sweetest sound,
    Whose tunes did far excel,
Full pleasantly and most profound
    Was all things placed well.
Thy pretty tune, mine own sweet bird,
    Done with so good a grace,
Extols thy name, prefers the same
    Abroad in every place.

Thy music grave, bedecked well
    With sundry points of skill,
Bewrays thy knowledge excellent,
    Engulfed in thy will.
My tongue shall speak, my pen shall write,
    In praise of thee to tell.
The sweetest bird that ever was,
    In friendly sort, farewell.

A SNOWY DAY

(translated from the Welsh by H. Idris Bell)

I cannot sleep or take the air –
Of a truth this load is hard to bear!
Ford or slope is none to be found,
Nor open space, nor bare ground.
No girl's word shall tempt me now
Out of my house into the snow.
The plaguey feathers drifting down
Like dragon's scales cling to the gown,
And all I wear would soon be
White as miller's coat to see.
Trus 'tis, the Winter Calends gone,
Ermine's the wear for everyone;
In January's month, first of the year,
God makes hermits everywhere.
Everywhere, the country round,
He has whitewashed the black ground,
Clothed in white each woodland glade,
On every copse a white sheet spread.

Like the white blossoms of April.
A cold veil on the forest lies,
A load of chalk crushes the trees.
Like wheaten flour the drifts appear,
A coat of mail that the plains wear,
A cold grit on field and fallow,
On earth's whole skin a thick tallow,
Foam-flakes flying thick and fast,
Fleeces big as a man's fist,
White bees of heaven on the wing,

Through all Gwynedd wandering.
Will God's plenty never cease –
So many feathers of holy geese,
Like winnowed chaff, heaped together,
A robe of ermine above the heather?
There in deep drifts the fine dust stays,
Where song was and the winding ways.
Who can tell me what folk they are
On the wintry earth spit from afar?
Heaven's white angels they must be
Busy about their carpentry.
The plank is lifted from the flour bin,
And down floats the flour within;
Silver cloaks of ice that pass,
Quicksilver, the coldest ever was,
A hampering chimer, white and chill,
Cement on hollow, ditch, and hill,
Earth's mail corslet, cold and hard,
A pavement vast as the sea's graveyard.
On all my land what monstrous fall,
From sea to sea a grey wall!
Who dare affront its rude domain?
A cloak of lead! – where is the rain?

FORGET-ME-NOT

When to the flowers so beautiful
    The Father gave a name,
Back came a little blue-eyed one
    (All timidly it came),
And standing at its Father's feet
    And gazing in His face,
It said in low and trembling tones

    With sweet and gentle grace,
'Dear God, the name Thou gavest me
    Alas! I have forgot.'
Then kindly looked the Father down,
    And said, 'Forget Me not.'

THE FAIRY SLEEP AND LITTLE BO-PEEP

Little Bo-Peep
Had lost her sheep,
And didn't know where to find them,
All tired she sank
On a grassy bank,
And left the birds to mind them.

Then the fairy, Sleep,
Took little Bo-Peep,
In a spell of dreams he bound her,
And silently brought
The flock she sought,
Like summer clouds around her.

When little Bo-Peep –
In her slumber deep –
Saw lambs and sheep together,
All fleecy and white,
And soft and light,
As clouds in July weather;

Then little Bo-Peep
Awoke from her sleep,
And laughed with glee to find them
Coming home once more,
The old sheep before,
And the little lambs behind them.

WHITHER SO FAST?

WHITHER so fast? See how the kindly flowers
    Perfume the air, and all to make thee stay.
The climbing woodbind, clipping all these bowers,
    Clips thee likewise for fear thou pass away.
    Fortune, our friend, our foe will not gainsay.
Stay but awhile, Phoebe no tell-tale is:
She her Endymion, I'll my Phoebe kiss.

Fear not, the ground seeks but to kiss thy feet.
    Hark, hark how Philomela sweetly sings,
Whilst water-wanton fishes, as they meet,
    Strike crotchet time amidst these crystal springs,
    And Zephyrus 'mongst the leaves sweet
    murmurings.
Stay but awhile, Phoebe no tell-tale is;
She her Endymion, I'll my Phoebe kiss.

See how the heliotrope, herb of the sun,
    Though he himself long since be gone to bed
Is not of force thine eyes' bright beams to shun,
    But with their warmth his goldy leaves unspread,
    And on my knee invites thee rest thy head.
Stay but awhile, Phoebe no tell-tale is;
She her Endymion, I'll my Phoebe kiss.

ANON-DE-SCRIPT

THE ALTO'S LAMENT

It's tough to be an alto when you're singing in
    the choir
The sopranos get the twiddly bits that people
    all admire,
The basses boom like loud trombones, the tenors
    shout with glee,
But the alto part is on two notes (or, if you're
    lucky, three).
And when we sing an anthem and we lift our
    hearts in praises
The men get all the juicy bits and telling
    little phrases.
Of course the trebles sing the tune – they always
    come off best;
The altos only get three notes and twenty-two
    bars rest.
We practise very hard each week from hymn-book
    and the Psalter,
But when the conductor looks at us our voices start
    to falter;
'Too high! Too low! Too fast – you held that note
    too long!'

It doesn't matter what we do – it's certain to
     be wrong!
Oh! shed a tear for altos, they're the Martyrs and
     they know,
In the ranks of choral singers they're considered
     very low.
They are so very 'umble that a lot of folk forget 'em;
How they'd love to be sopranos, but their vocal
     chords won't let 'em!

And when the final trumpet sounds and we are
     wafted higher,
Sopranos, basses, tenors – they'll be in the
     Heavenly Choir.
While they sing 'Alleluia!' to celestial flats and sharps,
The altos will be occupied with polishing the harps.

METHUSELAH

METHUSELAH ate what he found on his plate,
    And never, as people do now,
Did he note the amount of the calorie count;
    He ate it because it was chow.

He wasn't disturbed, as at dinner he sat,
    Destroying a roast or a pie,
To think it was lacking in lime or in fat,
    Or a couple of vitamins shy.

He cheerfully chewed every species of food,
    Untroubled by worries or fears,
Lest his health might be hurt by some fancy dessert –
    And he lived over nine hundred years!

THE VILLAGE CHOIR

Half a bar, half a bar,
Half a bar onward!
Into an awful ditch
Choir and precentor hitch,
Into a mess of pitch,
    They led the Old Hundred.
Trebles to right of them,
Tenors to left of them,
Basses in front of them,
    Bellowed and thundered.
Oh, that precentor's look,
When the sopranos took
Their own time and hook
    From the Old Hundred!

Screeched all the trebles here,
Boggled the tenors there,
Raising the parson's hair,
    While his mind wandered;
Theirs not to reason why
This psalm was pitched too high:
Theirs but to gasp and cry
    Out the Old Hundred.
Trebles to right of them,
Tenors to left of them.
Basses in front of them,
    Bellowed and thundered.
Stormed they with shout and yell,
Not wise they sang nor well,
Drowning the sexton's bell,
    While all the church wondered.

Dire the precentor's glare,
Flashed his pitchfork in air
Sounding fresh keys to bear
    Out the Old Hundred.
Swiftly he turned his back,
Reached he his hat from rack,
Then from the screaming pack,
    Himself he sundered.
Tenors to right of him,
Tenors to left of him,
Dischords behind him,
    Bellowed and thundered.
Oh, the wild howls they wrought:
Right to the end they fought!
Some tune they sang, but not,
    Not the Old Hundred.

FRANKIE AND JOHNNY

Frankie and Johnny were lovers,
    Lordy, how they could love.
Swore to be true to each other,
    True as the stars up above.
        He was her man, but he done her wrong.

Frankie went down to the corner,
    To buy her a bucket of beer,
Frankie says 'Mister Bartender,
Has my lovin' Johnny been here?
        He is my man, but he's doing me wrong.'
'I don't want to cause you no trouble,
    Don't want to tell you no lie.
I saw your Johnny half-an-hour ago
    Making love to Nelly Bly,
        He is your man, but he's doing you wrong.'

Frankie went down to the hotel
    Looked over the transom so high.
There she saw her lovin' Johnny
    Making love to Nelly Bly.
        He was her man; he was doing her wrong.

Frankie threw back her kimono,
    Pulled out her big forty-four;
Rooty-toot-toot three times she shot
    Right through that hotel door.
        She shot her man, who was doing her wrong.

'Roll me over gently,
    Roll me over slow,

Roll me over on my right side,
    'Cause these bullets hurt me so,
        I was your man, but I done you wrong.'

Bring all your rubber-tyred hearses
    Bring all your rubber-tyred hacks.
They're carrying poor Johnny to the burying ground
    And they ain't gonna bring him back,
        He was her man, but he done her wrong.

Frankie says to the sheriff,
    'What are they going to do?'
The sheriff he said to Frankie,
    'It's the 'lectric chair for you.
        He was your man, and he done you wrong.'

'Put me in that dungeon,
    Put me in that cell,
Put me where the northeast wind
    Blows from the southeast corner of hell.
        I shot my man, 'cause he done me wrong.'

BRIAN O'LINN

Brian O'Linn had no breeches to wear
He got an old sheepskin to make him a pair
With the fleshy side out and the woolly side in,
'They'll be pleasant and cool,' says Brian O'Linn.

Brian O'Linn had no shirt to his back,
He went to a neighbour's, and borrowed a sack,
Then he puckered the meal bag in under his chin –
'Sure they'll take them for ruffles,' says Brian O'Linn.

Brian O'Linn had no hat to put on,
So he got an old beaver to make him a one,
There was none of the crown left and less of the brim,
'Sure there's fine ventilation,' says Brian O'Linn.

Brian O'Linn had no brogues for his toes,
He hopped in two crab-shells to serve him for those.
Then he split up two oysters that match'd like a twin,
'Sure they'll shine out like buckles,' says Brian O'Linn.

Brian O'Linn had no watch to put on,
So he scooped out a turnip to make him a one.
Then he placed a young cricket in – under the skin –
'Sure they'll think it is ticking,' says Brian O'Linn.

Brian O'Linn to his house had no door,
He'd the sky for a roof, and the bog for a floor;
He'd a way to jump out, and a way to swim in,
''Tis fine habitation,' says Brian O'Linn.

Brian O'Linn went a-courting one night,
He set both the mother and daughter to fight;
To fight for his hand they both stripped to the skin,
'Sure I'll marry you both,' says Brian O'Linn.

Brian O'Linn, his wife and wife's mother,
They all lay down in the bed together.
The sheets they were old and the blankets were thin,
'Lie close to the wall,' says Brian O'Linn.

Brian O'Linn, his wife and wife's mother,
Were all going home o'er the bridge together,
The bridge it broke down, and they all tumbled in,
'We'll go home by the water,' says Brian O'Linn.

THE MAN ON THE FLYING TRAPEZE

Oh, the girl that I loved she was handsome,
I tried all I knew her to please.
But I couldn't please her a quarter as well
As the man on the flying trapeze.

Chorus:
> Oh, he flies through the air with the greatest of ease,
> This daring young man on the flying trapeze.
> His figure is handsome, all girls he can please,
> And my love he purloined her away.

Last night as usual I went to her home.
There sat her old father and mother alone.
I asked for my love and they soon made it known
That she-e had flown away.

She packed up her box and eloped in the night,
To go-o with him at his ease.
He lowered her down from a four-story flight,
By means of his flying trapeze.

He took her to town and he dressed her in tights,
That he-e might live at his ease.
He ordered her up to the tent's awful height,
To appear on the flying trapeze.

Now she flies through the air with the greatest of ease,
This daring young girl on the flying trapeze.
Her figure is handsome, all men she can please,
And my love is purloined away.

Once I was happy, but now I'm forlorn,
Like an old coat that is tattered and torn,
Left to this wide world to fret and to mourn,
Betrayed by a maid in her teens.

SIX IS A CROWD

Within my earthly temple there's a crowd:
There's one of us that's humble, one that's proud;
There's one that's broken-hearted for his sins,
And one who, unrepentant, sits and grins;
There's one who loves his neighbour as himself,
And one who cares for naught but fame and pelf –
From much corroding care I should be free,
If once I could determine which is Me.

ATHEIST'S HYMN

Lord, Lord, I don't believe in you,
I only believe in me.
Lord, your miracles I've never seen,
Only your earth and sea.
Lord, I know not your Heaven or Hell,
Only those which burn in me.
Lord, I wish to stand and shout from the hills,
Not mutter on bended knee.
Lord, Lord, I have only one prayer,
Which I cry irreverently:
Let me make music all my life long
Which reminds men of thee.

THE DOCTOR PRESCRIBES

A lady lately, that was fully sped
Of all the pleasures of the marriage-bed
Ask'd a physician, whether were more fit
For Venus' sports, the morning or the night?
The good old man made answer, as 'twas meet,
The morn more wholesome, but the night more sweet.
Nay then, i'faith, quoth she, since we have leisure,
We'll to't each morn for health, each night for pleasure.

THE WRAGGLE-TAGGLE GIPSIES

THREE gipsies stood at the castle gate.
They sang so high, they sang so low,
The lady sate in her chamber late,
Her heart it melted away like snow.

They sang so sweet, they sang so shrill,
That fast her tears began to flow.
And she laid down her silken gown,
Her golden rings and all her show.

She plucked off her high-heeled shoes,
A-made of Spanish leather, O.
She would in the street, with her bare, bare feet;
All out in the wind and weather, O.

O saddle me my milk-white steed,
And go and fetch me my pony, O!
That I may ride and seek my bride,
Who is gone with the wraggle-taggle gipsies, O!

O he rode high, and he rode low,
He rode through wood and copses, too,
Until he came to an open field,
And there he espied his a-lady, O!

What makes you leave your house and land?
Your golden treasures for to go?
What makes you leave your new-wedded lord,
To follow the wraggle-taggle gipsies, O?

What care I for my house and my land?
What care I for my treasure, O?
What care I for my new-wedded lord,
I'm off with the wraggle-taggle gipsies, O!

Last night you slept on a goose-feather bed,
With the sheet turned down so bravely, O!
And tonight you'll sleep in a cold open field,
Along with the wraggle-taggle gipsies, O!

What care I for a goose-feather bed,
With the sheet turned down so bravely, O!
For to-night I shall sleep in a cold open field,
Along with the wraggle-taggle gipsies, O!

IF I KNEW

If I knew the box where the smiles are kept,
No matter how large the key,
Or strong the bolt I would try so hard –
'Twould open, I know, for me.
Then over the land and sea broadcast
I'd scatter the smiles to play,
That the children's faces might hold them fast
For many and many a day.

If I knew the box that was large enough
To hold all the frowns I meet,
I would like to gather them every one
From the nursery, school or street,
Then, folding and holding, I'd pack them in
And turning the monster key,
I'd hire a giant to drop the box
To the depths of the deep, deep sea.

AN OLD MAN DREAMS

An old man by the fire will dream of all
The little things he did when he was young
He will remember early walks among
The woods and fields, when barley was as tall
As he himself was then. He will recall
A thunderstorm, a poem, a linnet's song,
And cricket, too, and he will dream and long
For the sweet singing sound of bat and ball.
He will remember how he held a catch,
Or how he stayed two hours at the crease,
And by his stubborn effort saved the match
When none but he could still defend their wicket
Against such bowlers. Dreaming thus of cricket
While the fire crackles, he will be at peace.

IF ALL THE WORLD WERE PAPER

If all the world were paper,
And all the sea were inke;
And all the trees were bread and cheese,
What should we do for drinke?

If all the world were sand 'o,
Oh, then what should we lack 'o;
If, as they say, there were no clay,
How should we make tobacco?

If all our vessels ran 'a,
If none but had a crack 'a;
If Spanish apes eat all the grapes,
What should we do for sack 'a?

If fryers had no bald pates,
Nor nuns had no dark cloisters,
If all the seas were beans and pease,
What should we do for oysters?

If there had been no projects,
Nor none that did great wrongs;
If fiddlers shall turne players all,
What should we do for songs?

If all things were eternall,
And nothing their end bringing;
If this should be, then, how should we
Here make an end of singing?

TO SALLY, AT THE CHOP-HOUSE

Dear Sally, emblem of the chop-house ware,
As broth reviving, and as white-bread fair;
As small-beer grateful, and as pepper strong,
As beef-steak tender, as fresh pot-herbs young;
Sharp as a knife, and piercing as a fork,
Soft as new butter, white as fairest pork;
Sweet as young mutton, brisk as bottled beer,
Smooth as is oil, juicy as cucumber,
And bright as cruet void of vinegar.
O Sally! could I turn and shift my love
With the same skill that you your steaks can move,
My heart, thus cooked, might prove a chop-house feast,
And you alone should be the welcome guest.
But, dearest Sal, the flames that you impart,
Like chop on gridiron, broil my tender heart!
Which, if thy kindly helping hand be n't nigh,
Must, like an upturned chop, hiss, brown and fry;
And must at last, thou scorcher of my soul,
Shrink, and become an undistinguished coal.

PASSING BY

There is a Lady sweet and kind,
Was never face so pleased my mind;
I did but see her passing by,
And yet I love her till I die.

Her gesture, motion, and her smiles,
Her wit, her voice my heart beguiles,
Beguiles my heart, I know not why,
And yet I love her till I die.

Cupid is wingéd and doth range
Her country, so my love doth change:
But change she earth, or change she sky,
Yet will I love her till I die.

MOSES IN THE BULLRUSHES

'Moses in the bullrushes, all dressed up in swathe
Pharaoh's daughter found him when she went down
    to bathe.
She took him to the palace, said, 'I found him on
    the shore.'
Pharaoh winked his eye and said, 'I've heard that
    one before.'

Samson was an Israelite, a mighty man was he.
He fancied young Delilah, from a different tribe was she.
He loved her lissom figure and she loved his curly mop
So all he got was a short back 'n' sides and a little bit
    off the top.

190

Solomon and David lived most immoral lives
Spent their time a-chasing after other people's wives
The Good Lord took them both to task – it worked just
    like a charm
For Solomon wrote the Proverbs, and David wrote
    the Psalms.

DAHN THE PLUG-'OLE

A muvver was barfin' 'er biby one night,
The youngest of ten and a tiny young mite,
The muvver was pore and the biby was thin,
Only a skelington covered in skin;
The muvver turned rahnd for the soap orf the rack,
She was but a moment, but when she turned back,
The biby was gorn; and in anguish she cried,
'Oh, where is my biby? – The angels replied:
'Your biby 'as fell dahn the plug-'ole,
Your biby 'as gorn dahn the plug;
The poor little thing was so skinny and thin
'E oughter been barfed in a jug;
Your biby is perfectly 'appy,
'E won't need a barf any more,
Your biby 'as fell dahn the plug-'ole,
Not lorst, but gorn before.'

A NOBLE BOY

The woman was old and feeble and grey,
And bent with the chill of the winter's day;
The street was wet with the recent snow,
And the woman's feet were weary and slow.
She stood at the crossing and waited long,
Alone, uncared for, amid the throng.
Down the street, with laughter and shout,
Glad in the freedom of 'school let out',
Came the boys, like a flock of sheep;
Hailing the snow, piled white and deep.
Past the woman, so old and grey,
Hastened the children on their way,
Nor offered a helping hand to her,
So meek, so timid, afraid to stir.

At last came one of the merry troop –
The gayest boy of all the group;
He paused beside her, and whispered low,
'I'll help you across if you wish to go.'
He guided the trembling feet along,
Proud that his own were firm and strong.
Then back again to his friends, he went,
His young heart happy, and well content,
'She is somebody's mother, boys, you know,
Although she is old and poor and slow.
And I hope some fellow will lend a hand
To help my mother – you understand –

If e'er she be poor and old and grey,
When her own dear boy is far away.'
And 'somebody's mother' bowed low her head,
In her home that night, and the prayer she said
Was, 'God be kind to the noble boy,
Who is somebody's son, and pride, and joy.'

HYMN AND PRAYER FOR CIVIL SERVANTS

O, Lord, Grant that this day we come to no
    decisions, neither
run we into any kind of responsibility, but that all
    our doings
may be ordered to establish new departments, for
    ever and ever. Amen.

    O Thou who seest all things below,
    Grant that Thy servants may go slow,
    That they may study to comply
    With regulations till they die.

    Teach us, O Lord, to reverence
    Committees more than common sense;
    To train our minds to make no plan
    And pass the baby when we can.

    So when the tempter seeks to give
    Us feelings of initiative,
    Or when alone we go too far,
    Chastise us with a circular.

    Mid war and tumult, fire and storms,
    Give strength O Lord, to deal out forms.
    Thus may Thy servants ever be
    A flock of perfect sheep for Thee.

THE INCOME TAX

Oh what wonders, what novels in this age there be,
And the man that lives longest the most he will see;
For fifty years back pray what man would have thought,
That a tax upon income would be brought.
    Sing, tantara rara new tax.

We're engag'd in a war who can say but 'tis just,
That some thousands of Britons as laid in the dust,
And the nation of millions it's made shift to drain,
Yet to go on with vigour each nerve we will strain.
    Sing, tantara rara will strain.

From the peer so down to the mechanical man,
They must all come beneath our minister's plan,
And curtail their expenses to pay their share,
To preserve their great rights & their liberties dear.
    Sing tantara rara how dear.

If you've not 601, you'll have nothing to pay,
That's an income too small to take any away,
But from that to a hundred does gradually rise,
All above, nothing less than the tenth will suffice,
    Sing tantara rara one-tenth.

This tax had produc'd what most wish to conceal,
The true state of their income few love to reveal,
What long faces it's caus'd, and of oaths not a few
Whilst papers they sign'd for to pay in their due.
    Sing tantara rara long face.

PRAYER

Mathew, Mark, Luke and John,
Bless the bed that I lie on
Before I lay me down to sleep
I owe my soul to Christ to keep.
Four corners to my bed,
Four angels there aspread,
Two to foot and two to head,
And four to carry me when I'm dead.
I go by sea, I go by land,
The Lord made me with his right hand.
If any danger come to me,
Sweet Jesus Christ deliver me.
He's the branch and I'm the flower,
Pray God send me a happy hour,
And if I die before I wake
I pray the Lord my soul to take.

                                        Amen